E.M. DELAFIELD

(1890-1943) was born Edmée Elizabeth Monica de la Pasture. She adopted her pseudonym "E.M. Delafield", a loose translation of her French ancestral name, because of the popularity of her mother's numerous novels, written under the name Mrs Henry de la Pasture. Her father was Count Henry de la Pasture of Llandogo, Monmouthshire (his family had come to England after the French Revolution), and after his death her mother married Sir Hugh Clifford, in 1910. E.M. Delafield served as a V.A.D. in Exeter from 1914-1917 and was then appointed to the Ministry of National Services in the South-Western Region at Bristol where she served until the end of the First World War. Her first novel, *Zella Sees Herself*, was published in 1917 and she was to write a further three before marrying Major Arthur Paul Dashwood O.B.E., the third son of Sir George Dashwood, sixth baronet, in 1919. They spent two years in the Malay States, afterwards settling in Devon where they had two children.

E.M. Delafield had written eighteen books when she was asked by Lady Rhondda to contribute a serial of some kind for the weekly *Time and Tide*. The result was *Diary of a Provincial Lady* (1930) which made E.M. Delafield one of Britain's best-loved writers of the 30s. *The Provincial Lady Goes Further* was published in 1932 and in 1933 E.M. Delafield's American lecture tour was serialised in *Punch* and formed *The Provincial Lady in America* (1934). *The Provincial Lady in Wartime*, appeared in 1940, and Virago published an omnibus of all four Diaries in 1984.

E.M. Delafield's writing provided her with a necessary life-line as well as additional income. Herself a provincial lady, her writing combined elegance and wit with a deep interest in the lives and conditions of her class, an interest reflected in her role as a Justice of the Peace and her involvement with Women's Institutes.

Her other work includes *The War Workers* (1918), *Humbug* (1922), *What is Love?* (1928), *Women Are Like That* (1929), *Thank Heaven Fasting* (1932), *Nothing is Safe* (1937) and *No One Now Will Know* (1941). A regular contributor to *Punch* and *Time and Tide* she also wrote three plays, *To See Ourselves* (1930), *The Glass Wall* (1933) and *The Mulberry Bush* (1935). The first of these was a dramatisation of her novel *The Way Things Are* (1927, also published by Virago) and was staged in both London and New York. At the age of fifty-three, E.M. Delafield collapsed while lecturing in Oxford and died some weeks later at

VIRAGO
MODERN
CLASSIC
NUMBER

291

E. M. DELAFIELD

THANK HEAVEN FASTING

WITH A NEW AFTERWORD BY
PENELOPE FITZGERALD

Published by VIRAGO PRESS Limited 1988
Centro House, 20–23 Mandela Street, London NW1 0HQ.

First published in Great Britain by Macmillan & Co. 1932
Copyright E.M. Delafield 1932

Afterword Copyright © Penelope Fitzgerald 1988

British Library Cataloguing in Publication Data

Delafield, E.M.
   Thank heaven fasting.—(virago
   modern classics).
   Rn : Edmée, Elizabeth Monica de la Pasture
   I. Title
   823′.912[F]   PR6007.E33
   ISBN 0-86068-995-6

Printed in Great Britain by Cox & Wyman Ltd.,
of Reading, Berkshire

DEDICATED
TO
MARGARET RHONDDA

MY DEAR MARGARET,

You will probably requite this dedication with one of those charmingly grateful letters that you so well know how to write. Let me at once forestall you by saying that the gratitude is entirely on my side, and that this book is only a very small expression of it.

Again and again, I have found that the sincerity and strength of your own work, both in *Time and Tide* and elsewhere, have set a standard for mine. I wish I could feel that I had attained to it.

Apart from the fact of our friendship, that to me is so wholly delightful, you are the fitting person to receive the dedication of this book, for it has sprung out of many conversations that we have held together.

Please accept it, with my gratitude and admiration.

ELIZABETH M. DELAFIELD

CONTENTS

Book One

The Eaton Square Tradition

CHAPTER I

MUCH was said in the days of Monica's early youth about being good. Life—the section of it that was visible from the angle of Eaton Square—was full of young girls who were all being good. Even a girl who was tiresome and "didn't get on with her mother" was never anything but good, since opportunities for being anything else were practically non-existent.

One was safeguarded.

One's religion, one's mother, one's maid. . . . But especially one's mother.

Monica's mother was even more of a safeguard than most, for she was very particular. Monica was brought up at home —an only child—and was not allowed to make friends with any of the other little girls at the dancing-class or at Mac-Pherson's gymnasium unless *her* parents knew *their* parents, and all about them.

"You may ask the little Marlowes to tea on Saturday, darling, for a great treat," said Mrs. Ingram from time to time.

It was a pity, Monica felt, that it so often had to be the little Marlowes. Frederica was domineering and conceited, and Cecily was shy and dull. Besides, both of them were older than she was, and Monica did not enjoy being the youngest.

But as Mrs. Ingram so often said: "The little Marlowes will be very nice friends for you later on, when you come out. Their mother knows practically everyone in London, and you could be certain of meeting all the right people there."

Lady Marlowe, the twice-widowed mother of Frederica and Cecily, was very rich. She had a house in Belgrave Square, and entertained a great deal. Her first husband had been a German Jew, but her second husband, the father of Frederica and Cecily, had been English. So it was all right.

Monica realized, as she grew up, how important it was that one should meet all the right people, since it was only amongst the right people that a young girl could find the man she might hope to marry.

"My darling, never fall in love with a man who isn't quite, *quite*——" Mrs. Ingram had said, at intervals, from the time that Monica was fifteen.

Besides this perfectly definite and direct piece of advice that she often pondered over very seriously, the whole tradition of Monica's world was daily and hourly soaking into her very being, so that it became an ineradicable part of herself, never wholly to be eliminated again from her innermost consciousness.

She could never, looking backwards, remember a time when she had not known that a woman's failure or success in life depended entirely upon whether or not she succeeded in getting a husband. It was not, even, a question of marrying well, although mothers were pretty and attractive daughters naturally hoped for that. But any husband at all was better than none. If a girl was neither married nor engaged by the end of her third season it was usually said, discreetly, amongst her mother's acquaintances, that no one had asked her.

Monica, sent for to the drawing-room to help her mother pour out tea, or sitting demurely on the edge of a chair in someone else's drawing-room at an Afternoon, took in fragments of conversation.

"I hear the poor Salthavens are sending that girl of theirs out to India to stay with her sister. If she doesn't get engaged out there, she never will."

10

"It's always much easier abroad. . . . Besides, there's the long voyage out."

"Oh yes, a sea-voyage is always an opportunity. And I must say, if I were the girl's mother, I'd hurry on the wedding *at* once, even if she has to get married out there. It's much too risky to let them wait, and, perhaps, the girl comes home to get her trousseau and things, and meanwhile *he* may find somebody else. . . ."

"I quite agree. It's funny, that girl never having got off. She's quite pretty, too, and both the elder sisters married early."

"One can never tell."

And at that point Mrs. Ingram might glance, perhaps a little anxiously, at Monica, who was not yet really come out, so that it was impossible to tell whether she was going to be one of the lucky ones or not.

Good looks had nothing to do with it. Monica had been told that very often, and fully realized it. It was nice to be pretty, and men might admire one for it, but that alone didn't really *lead* to anything.

Mrs. Ingram had a horror, with which she had impregnated her daughter, of things that didn't really lead to anything.

"Never make yourself cheap, darling. It doesn't lead to anything, in the long run, to let a man know that you like him or want him to like you."

"Don't talk about being 'friends' with a young man, my pet. There's no such thing as a friendship between a girl and a man. Either he wants to marry you, or he doesn't. Nothing else is any good."

"A girl who gets herself talked about is done for. Men may dance with her, or flirt with her, but they don't propose. She gets left."

"Never have anything to do with a young man who's familiar—asking if he may call you by your Christian name, or write to you, or anything like that. A gentleman doesn't *do* those things to the kind of girl that he respects, and might want to marry."

11

Monica had heard these and similar maxims so very often that she had long ceased to pay conscious attention to them, and merely accepted them as being amongst the fundamentals of life.

At eighteen, she was presented at Court, and made her formal *début*.

Mrs. Ingram and Lady Marlowe, jointly, gave a ball for the Misses Marlowe and Miss Monica Ingram.

"Do you see, my darling, how wise I was to insist upon your making friends with Cecily and Frederica? Look what it's led to!" said Mrs. Ingram, triumphantly and tenderly both at once.

It led, amongst other things, to the most crowded three weeks that Monica's young life had hitherto experienced. The ball was to be given at the Ritz. Mrs. Ingram would have secretly much preferred it to take place at Lady Marlowe's house in Belgrave Square, but this the elder lady did not offer. She said that she intended to give one or two quite small dances there in the course of the season, and that was enough. "Certainly, those girls are having *every* chance," Mrs. Ingram said to Monica privately. "Lady Marlowe pretends that there's a man after Frederica, but I don't believe a word of it. If there is, why hasn't he proposed to her, and why isn't she engaged? She's nearly twenty-four."

Monica didn't believe a word of it, either, although Frederica occasionally made a pretence to the same effect. But she did so rather half-heartedly, as though aware that Monica had known her too long, and with too profound a schoolroom intimacy, to believe her when she was lying. Besides, Cecily, who never lied and who adored Frederica, had a way of turning white and looking miserable, when her sister was not speaking the truth, that gave the whole thing away.

Monica felt sorry for Frederica, and did not blame her for pretending to a non-existent conquest. A girl simply had to, for the sake of her own self-respect. Cecily never did— but then Cecily was quite unlike other girls. She seemed

12

immature and childish, although she was twenty-two years old, and she was completely dominated by Frederica.

Their mother was always saying how wonderful was their devotion to one another, but Monica thought that Frederica was a bully, and that Cecily would be happier if her elder sister got married.

Frederica, however, did not get married.

Monica couldn't help feeling that it really would be wonderful, and a great triumph, if she herself could get married before Frederica. Mrs. Ingram, too, when the date of the ball had been definitely settled, and just before the great rush of preparations for it began, said to her daughter:

"I must say, darling, it would be really rather funny, supposing you were to get engaged before either of the Marlowes. I don't see why something shouldn't happen. This ball is a wonderful start for you, and might lead to any number of really *good* invitations."

In the meanwhile, there was a tremendous amount to be done. A lady—she wasn't really a lady, naturally, but one called her so to the servants—came to Eaton Square, and was established at the writing-table in the back drawing-room, with piles of envelopes, gilt-edged invitation cards, and Mrs. Ingram's address-book, and set to work.

Mrs. Ingram was driven in the brougham between the Ritz and various florists, caterers, and other Bond Street establishments. She was having her tiara reset, and her rings cleaned, and Monica's pearl necklace restrung. There were also appointments to be made, and kept, with dressmakers, hairdressers, and milliners.

Mrs. Ingram did not take Monica to her own dressmaker. She had been told of a woman who was really wonderful for *jeunes filles*—Myrtle, in Hanover Street.

So to Myrtle they went.

"White, of course," said Mrs. Ingram to Monica. "And I'm going to have it of satin. It looks much more *comme il faut*. You might have a tiny little *diamanté* edging, perhaps."

13

"A pearl trimming is pretty," suggested Monica.

"Oh no, darling, I don't care for that nearly so much," said her mother.

So that settled that.

Madame Myrtle—a large, camomile-coloured person—was full of assurances about knowing exactly what Moddam meant, and said that she was always more interested in a coming-out dress than in any other. She showed Mrs. Ingram a number of designs, and one or two models, and finally Monica was directed to come into the fitting-room and try on one or two evening-dresses, "just to see." In the tiny cubicle behind pink plush curtains there was just room for Mrs. Ingram, sitting on a little gilt chair, Monica standing before the long mirror on the wall, and Madame Myrtle, half in and half out of the recess, an arm extended behind her to receive the dresses brought by an assistant.

"Can Mam'zelle manage? We're hoping to move into larger premises in the autumn. . . . I'm really sorry you're so cramped, Mam'zelle."

"It's all right. If you'll just unfasten me at the back, mother."

Mrs. Ingram dealt competently by Monica's hooks and eyes. The girl stepped out of her dress and took off her flower-wreathed hat—pink roses and green leaves. It was a pity that one's hair always became so untidy under a hat. Monica's brown hair was soft and straight, and very fine, and it fell in untidy wisps round her face. She hastily pushed some of the ends back, trying to tuck them under the pad that, pinned to the back of her head, supported two little rows of sausage curls. Then she untied the blue ribbons of her embroidered camisole, unfastened it, took off her white petticoat and pulled down her thick chemise, rucked up under her heavily boned, tightly laced stays. Her black lisle-thread stockings and patent-leather shoes looked incongruous, coming below all the white underclothing—but they wouldn't show, once the dress was on.

"There!"

A pale-blue satin evening-dress, the round *décolletage* edged with very pale-pink velvet pansies, was carefully put over her head, whilst Madame Myrtle herself guided Monica's uplifted hands and arms into the short sleeves.

"Oh *no*," said Mrs. Ingram instantly. "I shouldn't dream of letting her wear colours yet. She's much too young."

"But, of course, Moddam," returned Madame Myrtle reproachfully, "this is simply for the style. I should never think of suggesting anything but white or ivory, or perhaps the very palest pink, for a *débutante* like Mam'zelle. I only wished Moddam to judge the general style."

"Oh, I see. Well—turn round, Monica."

Monica turned obediently, although the double rows of hooks and eyes, one on the lining and the other on the dress itself, were not yet fastened.

Madame Myrtle's thick, cold fingers set deftly to work, and meanwhile Monica looked at herself in the glass.

She thought it was a pity that her mother would not allow her to wear coloured evening-dresses. It seemed to her that they suited her very well indeed. Pink would probably be even better for her than blue, because her eyes were brown, and her face naturally rather pale. She wished, not for the first time, that her nose had been short instead of aquiline and rather long—but the wish was tinged with a slight feeling of guilt, for her mother had told her that it was a foolish one, and that an aquiline nose was very much more distinguished-looking than a short one. Monica still remembered how, at fifteen, she had tried to argue the point, and her mother had said very quietly:

"Darling, who knows best—you or mother?"

Convicted thus of her own presumption, Monica had naturally found nothing further to say.

"Her Presentation frock had a V-shaped neck . . . she's rather inclined to collar-bones just at present. . . . Monica, hold yourself up. Put your shoulders back properly."

Monica hastily obeyed.

She was feeling tired already, but two more dresses had to be tried on before her mother and the dressmaker finally decided to have one of them copied in white satin, with a V-shaped *décolletage* and a kind of stole or scarf of white tulle draped over either shoulder, to fall down the front of the dress and end in large tassels of silver cord.

"What flowers is Mam'zelle going to carry? Roses?"

"Lilies of the valley," said Mrs. Ingram decidedly. "They look so pure and sweet, just as a young girl ought to look.

"Now, as to cost. You know, I shall bring her here for other things if I'm pleased with this, so I hope you can manage rather a special price for me."

"I'll get you out an estimate at once, Moddam, and keep it as moderate as I possibly can. You see, it's the quality of the satin—you wouldn't want anything but the very best——"

"No, certainly not," said Mrs. Ingram. "Still—— Monica, darling, hurry up and dress, and then run along and wait for me. You can put your hat on in the shop."

Monica neither liked being told to run along, nor having to put her hat on in the shop, but there was no help for either. She did as she was told, and then waited for her mother. Mrs. Ingram did not keep her waiting very long. There was far too much to be done.

Almost every day there were fittings, for one thing or another, and various purchases to be made, and orders to be given to tradespeople, and consultations with Lady Marlowe. Whilst these last went on, Monica was usually sent upstairs to find Frederica and Cecily; for it was always Mrs. Ingram who went to Lady Marlowe's house in Belgrave Square.

One afternoon, two days before the ball, Monica went up to the sitting-room shared by the sisters on the third storey.

"May I come in?"

"Hullo, Monica!"

Frederica, moving awkwardly, got up and kissed her. Cecily kissed her also, but said nothing. She was like a pastel copy of her sister—pale where Frederica was brightly tinted, and with very light hazel eyes instead of dark-grey ones, and ash-blonde hair instead of chestnut. Both were very tall and stooped badly, both had curious dark shadows beneath their eyes, lax mouths that drooped a little, and long, pale, inefficient hands. Neither was ever wholly natural or free from self-consciousness, but Frederica's constraint took the form of an aggressive self-assertion, and Cecily's of an almost complete withdrawal into herself. They achieved a semblance of ease with Monica, provided always that their dominating and intensely vital mother was not present.

"Can I stay here for a little while? Mother's downstairs."

"Of course. Come and sit down. Are you getting excited about your first ball?"

"Oh, very. I only hope I shan't be a wallflower the whole evening."

"I'll introduce as many men as I possibly can to you," volunteered Frederica.

"Thanks very much, Fricky, but I daresay I shall know a good many there already," Monica retorted, her false humility vanishing in the light of Frederica's patronage.

"You've no idea how quickly men get all their dances booked up. Of course, I know they'll have to ask us, on Thursday night, because we're the daughters of the hostesses. But quite often a man has such a lot of duty dances to get through that he simply can't ask one."

"He could if he wanted to enough."

"You haven't been out long enough to understand," said Frederica coldly.

Cecily was twisting her hands about uneasily. Anything that seemed, however distantly, to threaten an emotional disturbance, had a most curious effect on her. She dreaded it to a degree that affected her physically, making her turn whiter than ever, and begin to shake.

Monica was conscious, now, of tension in the atmosphere. It was almost always there with Frederica and Cecily, and more especially in their own home. Sometimes there seemed to be no specific cause for this, sometimes it was a cause so trivial as to be almost unbelievable. Very often, it was due to Frederica's frenzied and possessive solicitude for her sister. Cecily was delicate, and Frederica would never let her, or anyone, forget it.

"I think Cecily's starting a cold," she said now, her face suddenly falling into exaggeratedly tragic curves.

"I don't think I am," Cecily said. Her eyes looked terrified, as though the issue was one of great magnitude. It was, indeed, obvious that it was so to the sisters.

"You always say that." Frederica was suddenly tense with fury. "If only you'd say *at once* when anything was the matter —but you always go on and on, saying it's nothing."

Cecily turned her scared gaze imploringly on Monica, as though to ask "Can you wonder at it?" But she said nothing.

"Perhaps you can stifle it, if it *is* a cold, till after Thursday," suggested Monica. She could see the relief on Cecily's far too expressive face at this lightening of the subject.

But Frederica could not let it go.

"You don't know what Cecily's colds are like," she said darkly. "You think it's just an ordinary cold, that's over in three days. But with her, it may go on her chest at any moment, and mean nights and nights of coughing——"

They couldn't stop her, although both of them had heard her say the same thing many times before.

Monica shrugged her shoulders, but Cecily looked as though she might be going to faint.

There was a knock at the door, and the footman, young and trim in black livery with yellow facings, stood on the threshold.

"If you please, her Ladyship wishes the young ladies to come to the drawing-room."

"Thank you, William. Is it a visitor?"

18

"Yes, Miss Frederica. Mr. Pelham is here."

"Who's Mr. Pelham?" enquired Monica, as William shut the door behind him.

"Oh, he often comes to dinner. He's a friend of mamma's, a barrister. It's very useful, knowing him, because he isn't married, and she can usually get him when she wants an extra man."

"Mother says that Lady Marlowe is perfectly wonderful about men. She *always* has enough."

"I know," said Frederica. She did not look as triumphant as she should have looked, and Monica dimly guessed why. Lady Marlowe, witty and vivacious, and still handsome, attracted men. That was why they came to Belgrave Square. Not for any other reason.

"Do you suppose we're all expected to go down?" asked Cecily.

"William seemed to think so. But I should think *you'd* much better stay in one atmosphere. It's much warmer in the drawing-room than it is up here, and you'll only feel the difference afterwards."

"Come on," said Monica impatiently. "The way you fuss, Fricky! It's absurd. I can't think why Cecily stands it. She ought to tell you to mind your own business. She's old enough to look after herself."

Monica went out of the room, not looking at Frederica. She knew that to suggest rebellion on Cecily's part was to attack Frederica where she was utterly and helplessly vulnerable. Her furious possessiveness could brook no hint of a possible thwarting.

On the landing outside the double-doors of the drawing-room, all three paused for a moment and, quite unconsciously, assumed entirely new and artificial expressions before going in.

Monica put her shoulders back, and raised her chin, the echo of countless adjurations to "hold up" returning automatically to her mind, as it always did in the presence of either of her parents.

19

Frederica and Cecily did not do the same. Both were intensely conscious of their height, and stooped partly from the wish to minimize it, partly from sheer lack of vitality. They gave limp and chilly hands to the greeting clasp of the visitor, and withdrew from the contact quickly, obscurely disliking it.

Mr. Pelham was introduced to Monica.

Already, before entering the room at all, indeed from the moment that she had heard he was unmarried, something that lay far below the layers of conscious thought, had asked the never dormant question: "Will he——?"

Mr. Pelham did not look young. He was heavily built, with a dark moustache, thinning dark hair, and rather prominent brown eyes. Still, he was tall and smiled agreeably as Monica shook hands with him. She noticed that he did not smile at Frederica or Cecily.

"Fricky, darling," said Lady Marlowe, "I want you to go and send a telephone message for me. Go and fetch a half-sheet of notepaper and a pencil from the writing-table, and put down just what I tell you."

Lady Marlowe's instructions were always explicit.

She looked very smart and bright and sparkling in her green afternoon dress, with a diamond butterfly pinned to the front of it, and her brown hair curling neatly under the almost invisible mesh of the hair-net.

As Frederica obeyed, an almost imperceptible nod and glance from her mother sent Cecily to sit by Mrs. Ingram, to make polite conversation about the ball.

Monica realized that she, the visitor, was to be given the chance of talking to the only man present.

Evidently he realized it too, for he made a slight gesture as of pushing forward one of the many small arm-chairs that stood about in pairs, between silk-shaded standard lamps, small tables crowded with framed photographs, and still smaller tables destined to support, at the most, a stray tea or coffee cup.

Monica sat down, and Mr. Pelham sat down, carefully

drawing up the knees of his dark-grey striped trousers as he did so.

"Have you been to the Academy yet?" said Mr. Pelham.

"Yes, twice. Have you?"

"Not since the Private View. Were you there then?"

"No. We went on the Opening Day. It was terribly crowded."

"I expect it must have been. It still is, I believe."

"Yes, I expect so. In fact, it was, the second time we went."

"When was that?"

"About ten days ago. My father took me. It was very crowded then. I mean, there were crowds of people there."

"I expect there were. Did you like any of the portraits?"

"I liked the Sargeants," said Monica, knowing that this was the right thing to say.

"Yes, they're good, aren't they?"

Mr. Pelham, at this point in the conversation, was obliged to get up and open the door for Frederica, who had received her mother's instructions and was going downstairs to the telephone.

Monica, glancing swiftly round, caught the gleam of approval in her mother's tiny smile.

She had succeeded in sustaining her conversation with Mr. Pelham without any of those pauses that might have indicated that he was finding her something less than interesting. Monica fixed her eyes upon him, as he closed the door behind Frederica, and tried to look as though taking it for granted that the break in their duologue had been a temporary one merely.

But there was an empty chair next to Lady Marlowe's corner of the sofa . . . he might go and take that. Monica redoubled her alertness of her gaze. Almost, she had her lips parted, as if just about to speak.

Mr. Pelham closed the door carefully, turned round, hesitated for the fraction of a second, and then returned to his place next to Monica.

She was careful not to glance away from him, but she could feel her mother's imperceptible sigh of relief.

Monica knew that her mother was pleased with her, and she was pleased with herself.

It looked as though she might be going to turn out attractive to men.

CHAPTER II

ON THURSDAY afternoon, before the ball, Monica was told by her mother to go upstairs and lie down.

"Otherwise you won't look fresh for to-night, darling. And the hairdresser's coming at seven o'clock. He can do me first, and then you."

"I shan't sleep," protested Monica.

"Never mind. You'll be resting. Now let me see——"

Mrs. Ingram consulted a list. She had been entirely absorbed in lists during the past three weeks.

"Let me see . . . cards for the dinner-table, yes, that's done . . . speak to Mrs. Horben about the salted almonds . . . telephone to the Stores—now what was that for, I wonder—send round to Gunter's about the ice-pudding— Monica, what are you hanging about for? I told you to go and lie down."

"Can't I help you, mother?"

"You can help me best by doing what you're told, *directly* you're told," said Mrs. Ingram firmly.

Monica went upstairs.

She did wish that her mother would not talk to her as though she were still a child. Once, she had ventured to say so, in a moment of intimacy, and Mrs. Ingram had kissed her and answered gently: "To me, you can never be anything but my baby, even if you live to be a hundred."

To the irrational tenderness of such a declaration, no dutiful and affectionate daughter could make any reply.

Monica's bedroom was on the fourth floor, a flight of stairs higher than that of anybody else—except, of course, the servants, who didn't count. They were at the very top of the house, next door to the boxroom. Indeed, Monica had a dim idea that the kitchen-maid actually did sleep in the box-room, but dressed and undressed with one of the other maids, in another room. Her window looked out on to the Square, and she gazed down for a moment at the striped awning already lowered over the balcony. It hid from her any view of the street, but she knew that another awning was in process of being put up, at the front door, and that strange men in dirty white aprons were hurrying up and down the steps, carrying in cardboard boxes and pots of azaleas and smilax.

Really, the ball might almost have been taking place at Mrs. Ingram's own house. But it was only a dinner-party before the ball.

Monica slowly drew the green blind half-way down between the rose-pink silk curtains, filling the room with a soft, summery gloom.

The pink silk eiderdown quilt had already been turned back over the brass rail at the foot of the bed, and the crisp, smooth linen sheet folded a little away from the pillow. Evidently Mary, the housemaid, had guessed that Miss Monica would be told to rest, before the tremendous excitement of the evening. Slowly Monica began to undress. Sometimes, in order to save herself trouble, she tried to lie down without taking off her stays, but it was never endurable. In the same way, it wasn't worth while trying to avoid the business of taking one's hair down. The hairpins hurt, and sooner or later they fell out, and, in any case, it had all to be done again as soon as one got up.

So Monica went to the dressing-table, and took down her hair altogether, laying the thick black hairpins, and the thin "invisibles" into two tidy little heaps beside the pad that supported her sausage-curls. Hastily she brushed back her hair, wishing that it were longer—it only reached to her shoulders—and plaited it in a small tail. For a moment or two she gazed earnestly at the reflection in the glass.

The Viyella nightgown—her mother did not think anything but Viyella really ladylike—thick things in the winter and thin in the summer—made her look very childish, with its little frills at neck and wrists, and neat row of buttons down the front. It was cut so as to fall in ample folds, and reminded Monica of a choir-boy's surplice. Moved by a sudden, incomprehensible impulse, she drew it tightly round her from the back, until the outline of her figure—rounded breasts, flat waist, and curving hips—was startlingly visible.

Shame assailed her, and she released the flannel folds abruptly and sprang into bed.

Anxious not to analyse her own immodest impulse, and indeed to forget it as quickly as might be, Monica looked round her room, consciously dwelling on the decoration, the arranging and furnishings that she and her mother had decided upon together as soon as Monica "grew up."

The wallpaper was a pattern of pink roses, crawling luxuriantly in and out of a silver-grey trellis work. Monica was not entirely satisfied with it. Her first idea had been to have a yellow room, but neither her father nor her mother had thought that at all a good idea, so that it had had to be abandoned. Still, after all, pink was pretty.

The china on the wash-stand was pink—little bouquets of roses tied with pink ribbon, on a white background—and the mats of the dressing-table were of pink Roman satin, covered with white spotted muslin. One lay beneath each of the bottles, brushes, trays, and boxes belonging to the embossed silver "dressing-table set" that Monica's father had given her on her sixteenth birthday. The back of each silver piece showed a raised reproduction of Sir Joshua Reynolds' "Heads of Angels."

The furniture itself was all painted white, so was the narrow little mantelpiece on which stood the collection of china animals, dating from nursery days. The pictures were framed in gilt—mostly "copies from the flat" of Swiss scenery, and Italian peasantry, but there were also reproductions of one or two "really *good*" pictures. These had been given to Monica from time to time, usually on birthdays, and she always felt that she ought to have liked them much better than she really did.

Her books, in a small open bookcase by the bed, she viewed with a much more real satisfaction. There was a set of Dickens, a set of Scott, a set of Ruskin, and several volumes of poetry. The storybooks—she was a little bit ashamed of all the L. T. Meades, and the Fifty-two Stories for Girls series—Monica still kept in the schoolroom. She was allowed, now, to read the books from Mudie's in the drawing-room, provided that she asked her mother's leave first, as to each one. The most individual thing in the room, Monica always felt, was the large coloured picture of the Emperor Napoleon that hung over the fireplace.

She had bought it with her own money, after deciding that Napoleon was her favourite hero. Mrs. Ingram had not, at first, been very pleased at this act of independence. She had not, however, forbidden the hanging of the picture, saying only: "It's a phase, darling. All girls go through it, I suppose."

Monica had felt foolish, but had stuck to Napoleon. She liked the feeling of having originated a cult for herself.

Beside the bed stood a little table with a framed photograph of Monica's father and mother, taken almost before she could remember them, a Bible and Prayer-book, and a copy of the Imitation of Christ, bound in limp green leather. A reproduction of the Sistine Madonna hung over the bed.

There had been a moment when Monica, really doubtful whether she was not at heart an atheist, had wished to take this down, and to substitute yet another Napoleon, but she had never found courage to do anything so entirely likely to lead to disaster. Besides, it wouldn't have been of any use. She would never have been allowed to take down the Madonna and Child. And after all, it was—like the pink wallpaper—very pretty, and reminded her of her childhood.

In these virginal surroundings, Monica lay and thought about her first ball.

She was deeply excited.

Nobody knew what might happen at a first ball.

There were stories about girls who had received proposals at their first balls, or even actually become engaged. Mrs. Ingram had many times told her daughter of the almost historic case of the aunt of Frederica and Cicely.

"She was Claire Bell—the youngest of all the family—and she went to her first ball when she was seventeen. She was very pretty, as they all were, and, of course, she had the advantage of two sisters who were already out, and could introduce men to her. Well, Sir Felix Craner saw her, and asked to be introduced, and he danced with her once or twice, and the *very next morning* he called on her father, and asked if he might propose. You can imagine how delighted the Bells were—three daughters still unmarried, and they weren't at all well off. And Claire married this very rich man before she was eighteen! Of course," Mrs. Ingram was apt to conclude the story with a sigh, "things like that don't happen every day."

"She must have been awfully pretty."

"She *was* pretty, I must say. But it isn't always prettiness that does it. As a matter of fact, Claire lost her looks very soon after. Still, what did that matter? There she was, married and settled at seventeen."

It seemed an almost unrealizable ideal.

One could not hope to be as brilliantly successful as all that. Still, it would be glorious to dance every dance, and to feel that one's partners were admiring one's dress, and one's dancing, and one's looks. Monica knew that she was, for instance, prettier than either Frederica or Cecily, who were both so much too tall, and held themselves so badly. It certainly was not *only* because she was a visitor that Mr. Pelham had talked so much more to her than to either of them. Mr. Pelham might be elderly, and not very good-looking, but still, he was a man.

Monica, dozing, dreamed that she was wearing an engagement ring, and that Frederica was jealous.

At four o'clock, her mother's maid brought her a cup of tea and a plate of sponge-fingers.

Parsons was good-natured, and fond of Monica. Otherwise she would certainly never have stumped up from the pantry, right down in the basement, but would have sent Mary.

"Thank you very much, Parsons," said Monica politely. She sat up in bed.

"What's mother doing?"

"Resting, Miss Monica. She's been on her feet all day long, and the master's just come in, and said she was to have a lay-down if it's only for half an hour."

"Oh, is father downstairs?"

"Yes, Miss Monica. He's just come in," repeated Parsons.

"Well, I should think I might get up now, and go downstairs, wouldn't you? The hairdresser isn't coming till seven."

"I don't know what madam's orders were, Miss Monica, but if she didn't say nothing special, then I should think you might go down."

"It isn't as if I hadn't had a doze. I went right off. I know I did, because I had a dream."

Monica gave a self-conscious little laugh, at the remembrance of the dream.

She had an absurd feeling that a dream like that might be a kind of good omen. It might even mean that she really *was* going to be engaged quite soon.

"Can I help you, Miss Monica?"

"No, thank you, Parsons. I can manage."

"Then, please Miss, could I come and fasten your dress for you not a minute later than half-past six?"

"But the hairdresser?"

"You'll want your dress on before he does your hair, Miss Monica, otherwise you'll never be able to get it over your head safely."

"No, of course, I shan't. All right, I'll be up here at half-past six."

Twenty minutes later, Monica ran down to the drawing-room, pausing for a moment to admire the gilt pot of marguerites that had suddenly appeared on a small table on the drawing-room landing, just below the pleated pale-blue curtains of the window. Then she opened the door and went in.

Her father stood by the window, as usual agreeably doing nothing. Presumably his occasional activities at the Bank of which he was a director exhausted Vernon Ingram's energies, for, outside the hours of business, he was seldom seen to do anything at all. Good-looking and imperturbable, he merely existed, politely and blandly, knowing everybody whom he considered to be worth knowing, and never making a mistake as to those who might, or might not, be included in the category. He smiled when he saw Monica, and lightly brushed her face with his pointed brown moustache.

"This is a great occasion, eh?"

"I'm awfully excited," exclaimed Monica. She would have said something of the kind, even had it been less than perfectly true, knowing that he expected it of her. Her relations with her father were almost entirely governed by her knowledge of what he would expect.

"That's right," Ingram murmured approvingly. "Mother has gone to have a little rest before dressing. She's been doing a very great deal lately, and we mustn't let her knock herself up, eh?"

"No, of course not."

Monica assumed an expression of dutiful concern, but in reality a faint, familiar pang of vexation shot through her, as it always did at every fresh proof of her father's solicitude for her mother.

It was not that she was so especially devoted to her father. Monica believed herself to love her mother better than anybody else. But there was a feeling of resentment, that she never sought to define, at knowing her mother to be the object of an exclusive affection such as Monica herself could not, as yet, claim from anyone.

"Have you been to play whist at the Club, father?"

The question dated from Monica's nursery days. She asked it several times weekly, and never realized that the reply was a matter of complete indifference to her.

"Yes, I had a couple of rubbers. One or two people were very amused to hear that I was taking my daughter to her coming-out ball to-night."

"Why?" asked Monica innocently.

Vernon Ingram laughed self-consciously.

"Perhaps they didn't quite realize that I *had* a grown-up daughter," he suggested.

Monica did not altogether understand. She often rode in the Park with her father, and had met a number of his friends. Why should they have failed to realize that of course she was grown-up?

But she said, "Oh, I see!" and laughed a little.

"I hope the new frock has arrived safely, and that you and your mother are very pleased with it all," said Ingram kindly.

"Very pleased, thank you, father."

"I want you to realize, dear child, that father and mother have taken a very great deal of trouble, and gone to a lot of expense, over this ball. Your mother, especially—I'm quite afraid that she's worn herself out."

"Oh, I hope not!" interjected Monica uncomfortably. Her father held up a long, beautifully shaped hand, and she perceived that she had interrupted him.

"You mustn't think that because Lady Marlowe is—is joining forces with us to-night that the brunt of it has not fallen upon your dear mother. It has. Naturally, we don't grudge any of it—we want you to have everything that we can give you. And I'm sure that you realize that, and will never—never disappoint us, in any way."

"No, father, I won't."

"That's right, darling. We hope that you're going to make a number of very nice friends, and prove that we were quite justified in this—this expense, and trouble, over your first ball."

30

"I can't thank you and mother enough, I know," murmured Monica.

Her father waved her embarrassed gratitude aside.

"We don't want any thanks, dear child. We just want you to enjoy yourself, and be a good, happy little girl. I'm looking forward to seeing you in your new dress to-night, very much indeed. You've had a little talk with your mother, as to dancing with people whom we know, and like, and not too many times with any one partner, eh?"

"Yes, father, mother has told me."

"That's right, that's right. I'm sure you'll be a very good child, and enjoy yourself very much. Have you seen anything of your friends, Frederica and Cecily, to-day?"

"Not to-day, father. I shall to-night, of course."

"Yes, yes. Well, we must see if you can't cut them both out in looks and dancing and everything else," said Ingram with simplicity. Then he sat down and took up the new *Cornhill Magazine*, and Monica perceived that the conversation was over.

She picked up a book from the table, and pretended to be reading it, but was quite unable to fix her attention. Her father's last words, echoing the thought that was never really out of her own mind, thrilled her with its implication that she might achieve triumphs of masculine admiration beyond those accorded to others.

Every now and then she looked anxiously up at the enormous ormulu clock on the marble mantelpiece, and its hands seemed to her to be moving so slowly that she several times wondered whether it had stopped.

At last, however, it was six o'clock and she could go up to her room again, and begin to dress.

It was really *beginning*.

Presently she was sitting in her white frilled flannel dressing-gown, waiting for Parsons. The new white satin dress lay on the bed, and on the floor were pointed, high-heeled, white satin shoes, that Monica knew only too well would hurt her long before the end of the evening.

There was a knock at the door, and she called "Come in!"

"*Now*, Miss!" said Parsons, full of sympathetic excitement.

Monica took off her dressing-gown, and the white satin dress was carefully lifted over her head, whilst she held her hair out of the way with one hand.

"Pin it up, Miss Monica—anyhow. Just to get it out of the way."

Monica drew in her breath while Parsons fastened the double rows of hooks and eyes, and smoothed down the ample skirts.

"There! It's lovely."

Monica had no long glass in her room. She surveyed herself in the mirror on the dressing-table, unable to keep herself from a smile of gratified pleasure and astonishment at the sight of her reflection, but saying to Parsons in as critical and detached a tone as she could command:

"It's not fair, of course, to judge with my hair not yet done. But I must say I think it looks very nice."

"Lovely, Miss Monica. And madam's silver sequins are beautiful, too. Now let me put on your dressing-gown again, miss, to keep everything quite safe. There! That's the bell. That'll be the hairdresser."

"Parsons! Ask if I can come in and sit with madam while he's doing her."

"Yes, Miss Monica."

In five minutes Parsons was back with the necessary permission, and Monica, with the dressing-gown gathered round her, and one hand carefully holding up the folds of the white satin beneath, had gone down to her mother's room.

Mrs. Ingram sat before the dressing-table, her head held motionless, whilst the tall, yellow-headed assistant from the Maison André Leroy in Sloane Street swiftly and vigorously twisted the hot irons in and out of her hair.

"Sit down, my pet. Are you all ready except for your hair?"

"Yes, mother."

"You're burning me—be *careful*——" squeaked Mrs. Ingram suddenly.

"I'm very sorry, madam, I beg your pardon." The young man, with an air of acute concern, snatched the tongs out of Mrs. Ingram's hair and held them up to his own face.

"I *beg* your pardon, madam. I don't think it's done any real harm, madam—the hair is not scorched. I'm extremely sorry it should have happened."

"Well."

The young man, looking deeply contrite, resumed his operations, and Mrs. Ingram muttered to her daughter:

"*Il est aussi stupide que possible.*"

Monica nodded intelligently.

"Darling, look on my writing-table, and you'll find a menu card. It's one I spoilt. Just read it through, and then you'll know how dinner is getting on, and be ready to jump up directly I catch Lady Margaret Miller's eye. It's such a bore if one person doesn't realize and goes on talking."

Monica fetched the stiff white card, with its narrow gilt edge, and read the items, although without any very great feelings of interest, from soups—thick and clear—turbot sauce madère, and sole meunière, entrée and joint, hot and cold sweets, savoury—canapés à l'Indienne, of course—to bombe glacée—which was the only item that aroused in her a faint anticipation of enjoyment.

"I see, mother. It ought to be very nice."

"Of course it'll be very nice, darling. I didn't ask you for your little opinion on the menu—what can you possibly know about it?" said her mother, laughing. "But you must learn how these things are done, of course. Directly dessert is finished, I shall make the move.

"Mr. Ashe will take you into dinner, and you'll have Lady Margaret's son, young Peter Miller, on the other side of you. The one you met at lunch the other day, at the Marlowes'."

"I don't remember which one he was," admitted Monica, with a confused recollection of a large Sunday lunch-party, and an indistinguishable herd of black-coated, grey-trousered men, and introductions performed in Cecily's shyest and most inaudible manner.

Mrs. Ingram made a sound with her tongue against the roof of her mouth, indicating dismay and disapproval.

"Darling, that's one of the things you'll have to learn— and as quickly as possible. You've *got* to remember who people are, and recognize them when you see them again, and not look blank and uninterested. A man is very quickly put off, if he thinks that a girl hasn't even taken the trouble to remember what he looks like."

"I'll try," said Monica meekly.

"Mr. Miller is in the Foreign Office, and he's the second son of Lady Margaret Miller, who was a Farren of Earls-wick, and an heiress. He'll be quite well off some day. The one who'll take you into dinner, and to whom you must talk most, of course, is Claude Ashe. His father and mother have a place in Wales, and very seldom come to London. I used to know his mother quite well, and she wrote and told me that this boy—he's the second son—was going to be in London for a bit. So I'm very glad to have a chance of doing something for him. Perhaps, if we like him, we could suggest his coming to a little theatre-party one night. Anyway, he'll call, after the dinner-party. You can let him know— and the other man too, of course—that I'm always at home on Sunday afternoons. Just mention it casually, you know."

"Very well, mother."

The hairdresser's work with the tongs was completed. He stepped backwards and surveyed Mrs. Ingram's reflection in the mirror with respectful admiration.

"Shall I dress it, madam?"

"My maid will do it, thank you, whilst you're waving the young lady.—Monica, run up to your room, darling, and —let me see—ring for Mary, and tell her that mother says she's to sit with you until Parsons is free."

Mary, the housemaid, was as busy as possible, but it was

clear that she must leave her work in order that Miss Monica should not be alone in her bedroom with the assistant from the Maison André and his curling-tongs. He, too, evidently appreciated the delicacy of the situation, for he did not knock at Monica's door until five minutes after Mary had breathlessly appeared there, and had been installed in a chair with a stocking to darn.

When Monica's hair had been tonged into waves of the stiffest and most uniform regularity, it was drawn backwards through the comb in order to fluff it out on either side of her head, and the ends were rolled into curls, and transfixed by two hairpins to the pad securely pinned on the back of her head. One or two short pieces of hair on the back of her neck were twisted up in the tongs until Monica winced in the apprehension of being burnt, and then the hairdresser silently handed her the looking-glass.

"Very nice indeed. Thank you so much," graciously said Monica, imitating her mother's phrasing and intonation of a kind especially reserved for such occasions.

"Thank you very much, Miss. Good evening, Miss."

He was gone, and Monica threw off her dressing-gown, and took the full effect of her appearance.

"It's lovely, Miss Monica. The dress suits you most beautiful," said Mary, with respectful warmth. "I'm sure there won't be a prettier young lady anywhere in the ball-room."

Monica's mother, sweeping into the room without warning, dismissed Mary to her duties downstairs, and inspected her daughter.

"Very nice—yes, very nice indeed, my darling. Hold yourself up—you don't want to poke like Frederica Marlowe. Let me see—you want a brooch just in front, there."

"I'll put on my blue swallow brooch."

"No, that won't do at all. You can't wear turquoises with a ball-dress. I'll lend you my little pearl heart. Just lean over the banisters, darling, and call to Parsons, and tell her to bring it up here. It's in my silver tray."

The brooch was found, and brought upstairs by Parsons, and Mrs. Ingram herself pinned it on the little white tulle edging of Monica's dress.

Then she said: "You want another hairpin—just *there*."

"Oh, mother, please let me put it in for myself," cried Monica impatiently.

"No, darling. You can't possibly tell where it's needed. Bend your head down."

Monica had to obey.

"That's perfect. Come along."

Mrs. Ingram, her dark head, with a diamond crescent twinkling on it, held high, preceded her daughter downstairs.

Vernon Ingram was waiting for them, standing in front of the flower-filled fireplace in the drawing-room.

"Well, well, well. Let's have a look at you. Turn round, Monica. . . . I declare, I'm very proud of my wife and my grown-up daughter."

He spoke lightly, but there was an emotional quality in the look with which he surveyed them. And it pierced, also, through the half-humorous tones of his voice, as he turned to his wife and indicated Monica by the smallest of gestures.

"I'm not sure, now that I look at her in full fig, that we shall be keeping her with us so very much longer, eh?"

CHAPTER III

Mr. Ashe was slight, tall, and very blond. His white eyelashes flickered a little when he spoke. Monica thought him nice-looking, and particularly liked his smile. It did not occur to her that he was shy, but she noticed, and was attracted by, the diffidence of his manner.

They began by exchanging the usual commonplaces of conversation, to which Monica was by this time getting accustomed. Later on, he asked her to keep some dances for him. Monica was startled and flattered, but mindful of her mother's injunction that to betray gratification at any advances from a man was to risk cheapening oneself, and thus lose his favour, she replied rather coldly that she did not think she would be able to dance until quite late in the evening.

"You see, my mother and Lady Marlowe are giving the ball, and I shall have to stay with them and help to receive people."

"Oh yes, of course. I see."

Rather to her disappointment, he said nothing more. Presently Monica, in response to a swift telegraphic look from her mother's end of the table, turned to her other neighbour, Mr. Miller, whom she had met at the Marlowes' and had not remembered.

She still did not remember him, for he seemed to her to look exactly like a number of other young men—dark and thin, with a nondescript face, and very little expression.

"I think we met at Lady Marlowe's house at lunch one Sunday," she began shyly.

Young Miller responded suitably, although without enthusiasm—he did not sound as though he would ever be enthusiastic about anything—and Monica did not find it difficult to sustain a conversation with him, continuous, even if rather disjointed owing to the rapidity with which they both seemed to come to an end of all that they had to say about the Academy, the season's dances, and such theatres as each had visited. It was with a little secret relief that Monica saw Mr. Miller, at a suitable pause, turn to the girl, unknown to Monica except as the daughter of one of her mother's friends, sitting on his other side. Mr. Ashe was still politely inclined towards his left-hand neighbour, a talkative and animated Mrs. St. George, whom Monica naïvely thought of as being necessarily uninteresting to young men because she had a thin, bald-headed husband sitting on the opposite side of the welter of smilax and red roses that lay all over the shining white of the tablecloth.

With a sense of drawing breath for a moment in the midst of some dangerous enterprise, Monica relaxed from the strain of being bright and animated, and looked about her.

Everybody seemed to be talking at once.

Lady Margaret Miller was laughing at something that her host was telling her.

The table looked lovely.

Monica herself was easily the youngest person in the room. It humiliated her slightly, to feel that this was so. Perhaps, however, her mother had done it on purpose. She always seemed to think it an asset, socially, to be young, although she also always emphasized to Monica the crudeness and ignorance of youth.

The ice-pudding was being handed round, followed by its accompanying *biscuits glacés*, little brown bundles tied together like faggots with red ribbon. The ice-pudding had come from Gunter's. Mrs. Horben could not have risen to such heights, although Monica's father always declared that her soufflés were incomparable. How did mother explain to Mrs. Horben, without hurting her feelings, that Gunter would have to supply the ice-pudding? Involuntarily Monica glanced towards the foot of the table. Mrs. Ingram was smiling and nodding, her whole attention apparently fixed upon the words of the grey-haired husband of Lady Margaret Miller. Yet, with scarcely the flicker of an eyelid—certainly without turning her head—she contrived to send a wordless injunction to her child.

Monica straightened her shoulders, drank some cold water, and addressed Mr. Claude Ashe once more.

"Do you know Lady Marlowe's two daughters—Frederica and Cecily?"

She was quite aware that he did, for she had heard Frederica mention his name, but she had not been able to think of anything else to say. However, it served to start a conversation again, and that was all that mattered.

Ten minutes later the eye of Lady Margaret Miller had been successfully caught by that of her hostess, and the ladies, rustling and tinkling and murmuring, had passed out of the door and were going up the stairs, Monica naturally coming last.

The comparative coolness of the hall and staircase came as a relief after the lengthy procession of courses in the dining-room, the blazing lights all round the room, and the strained excitement of making conversation.

There was the customary pause on the landing.

"Would you care to——? Monica darling, show Lady Margaret the way upstairs—— Would anyone else——? Yes, of course, Monica will show you. Turn on the light over my dressing-table, darling."

As if one wouldn't have thought of that without being told! Naturally people would want to powder their noses. Nearly every face was flushed and shining.

Monica seized an opportunity to fly upstairs to her own room and use her powder-puff vigorously. Heavens, it was only ten o'clock, and they weren't to start till eleven! It wouldn't have been as early as that, if her mother hadn't been one of the hostesses.

She hurried down again, and then sedately followed in the rear of the procession of descending ladies.

Mrs. Ingram had said:

"Before the men come up, after dinner, you must talk to one or two of the girls. It's the greatest possible mistake to think that it doesn't matter about making friends with other girls. It's *most* important. They can help you in all kinds of ways."

In one way especially, of course, Monica understood perfectly. It was through the good offices of other, slightly older, girls, that one might hope to meet young men.

Monica, reflecting thus, talked very readily to the other girls present, none of whom she knew very well. Lady Margaret Miller also spoke to her, and one or two of the elder ladies.

They all said the same thing.

"How do you like being grown-up?"

"Is this your first ball?"

One woman said: "My girl must introduce some of her partners to you. It makes such a difference," she added, as if half apologetically, to Monica's mother. "It makes such a difference, having been out a year or two. They've made their own friends by then."

"Of course," Mrs. Ingram agreed.

"It won't be long, I'm *sure*, before Monica has plenty of friends of her own."

They both laughed a little, but Monica felt that the eyes of her seniors had rested upon her with approval. She returned to make conversation with her contemporaries, all of them more or less covertly on the alert for the arrival of the men from the dining-room. When, however, the door at last opened, they talked to one another with added animation, and were careful not to turn round.

It seemed quite a long while before a general movement actually took place, and then, to her dismay, Monica found that she was still talking to another girl and that all the men seemed to be occupied with somebody else.

It was disappointing, and rather humiliating. Monica hoped, without much conviction, that her mother would not notice. However, it did not last long.

Lady Margaret Miller, very tactfully, said that it was a shame to keep the young things from their dancing, and that in any case she was sure dear Mrs. Ingram ought to be at the Ritz not a moment later than eleven o'clock.

There was an unconvincing demur from Mrs. Ingram, a general movement, and then Monica's father rang the bell and cabs and carriages were ordered. The brougham had been in waiting for nearly an hour.

"We shall meet later, then."

"I shall see you at the Ritz."

"I'll wait just outside the ball-room. It's been too delightful, coming here to-night. . . ."

"I hope you'll enjoy your first ball, Monica, and dance every single dance."

The party dispersed. Not all of them were going on to the ball. Some of the elder people had declined it and several others were due first at an Embassy reception.

"Now, Monica—let me have a look at you. Yes, very nice, darling. Your hair has kept in beautifully. Run upstairs and powder your nose and get your cloak, and we'll start at once."

In the brougham Mrs. Ingram was tense and preoccupied. Monica and her father talked to one another—but not very much.

"How did you get on at dinner, eh?"

"Quite well, thank you, father. I enjoyed it very much."

"That's right, my little girl. You looked very nice, and I thought you seemed to be having quite a pleasant time with our friends at the dinner-table."

Mentally translating, Monica knew this meant that she had not fallen into any awkward silences, but had contrived to keep the young men on either side of her engaged in conversation. She felt pleased, in spite of the acute sensation of suspense that was invading her more and more strongly as the climax of the evening approached.

"We're in very good time," said Mrs. Ingram abruptly. Monica could tell from her tone that she, too, was nervous. No wonder.

41

Almost directly, as it seemed, they were at the palm-and-flower decked entrance to the ball-room exchanging greetings with Lady Marlowe, superb and yet animated in her low-cut green satin, with an emerald tiara, emerald necklace, and large fan of white ostrich-feathers.

Frederica and Cecily hovered just behind her.

Frederica's dress was of pale blue with an edging of silver lace, and she held a bouquet of white roses. It was characteristic of her that the roses had already wilted in her limp grasp, and made a faint stain against the front of her dress.

Cecily was in white, and held a lace handkerchief and a small lace fan, instead of a bouquet. Her dress was more becoming than Frederica's, and she looked prettier than her sister. Her thick, beautiful fair hair curved away on either side of her brow with an effect as different as possible from that produced by the hard, regular undulations inflicted by the curling-irons on the heads of Monica and Frederica.

"How nice your hair looks, Cecily!"

"So does yours. Was the dinner-party fun?"

"Yes, quite. I sat between two men you know—Mr. Ashe and Mr. Miller."

"Peter Miller—oh yes. He's a sort of cousin of ours. Did you get on with him all right?"

"Oh, quite. I liked the other one better—Mr. Ashe. He asked me to keep some dances for him."

"Did he?" said Cecily, obviously impressed.

"Naturally," Frederica joined in. "Of course, everyone who dined at your house will ask you for at least two dances, Monica. They'll have to. I don't mean they won't want to, of course, but it's an understood thing."

Monica decided, not for the first time, that Cecily was much nicer than her sister.

"Here's the band," murmured Cecily, and at that moment Lady Marlowe called them to attention.

"Come along, girls! People will be arriving in a minute. You can chatter some other time. Now, remember: no dancing before twelve o'clock at the very earliest. I shall want you here, Frederica. It doesn't matter about you, Cecily —in fact, I think you'd better start dancing as soon as anyone asks you."

Lady Marlowe turned half apologetically towards Mrs. Ingram.

"Don't you think so? Three girls are really too many. Of course, Fricky and Monica must be here to say How d'y do; but Cecily is almost better out of the way—don't you agree?"

Mrs. Ingram, wording it politely, quite evidently did agree. Cecily retired to a little gilt chair inside the ball-room, and sat there looking very unhappy, until she was joined by the first arrivals.

Monica, standing close to her mother, heard Lady Marlowe say in the clear, amused voice that she kept for her most unkind sayings:

"My dear, be thankful that you've only one daughter. It's all right if the elder is safely married off before the younger one comes out; but if they're both hanging on at home together, it hampers one too *dreadfully*."

Monica did not look at Frederica, who must have heard.

She knew too well the look of sick humiliation that would come into her eyes, the slow tide of colour that would mount into her face.

Monica felt sorry for her.

"Darling, *wake up*!" hissed her mother.

People were beginning to arrive.

Monica put back her shoulders, smiled brightly, and fastened her white kid gloves preparatory to the exchange of a number of hand-shakes with other white kid gloves.

She heard all the names announced in an enormous, and yet modulated, shout by a strange man standing in the doorway, but people came so fast that she was not able to identify them. It was with quite a rush of astonished relief that she found herself facing white eyelashes, and a smile that seemed oddly familiar.

"Oh—Mr. Ashe!"

"What about those dances that you promised me? When may I have them?"

"I'm not to dance before twelve," she said doubtfully.

"Then the first waltz after twelve o'clock. I'll come for you here. Just the contrary of Cinderella!"

Monica found this amusing, and looked up at him and laughed. There was something agreeable in being obliged to look up at him, for she was tall enough to meet the eyes of most men on a level.

For a few minutes more Mr. Ashe stayed beside her, speaking to her very little, but, she felt, watching her. Monica became rather self-conscious, and tried to vary the tones of her stereotyped "How d'y do" and to shake hands at a new angle. Then, glancing round over her shoulder, she saw that he had passed on into the ball-room.

She wondered when it would be twelve o'clock. Soon, she hoped.

The stream of arrivals had stopped, and Lady Marlowe was sitting down, talking and laughing with a group of people, mostly men. *She* never had any difficulty in attracting, and keeping, the attention of men, thought Monica enviously.

Her own mother, her sequins glittering and her face becomingly flushed, was actually telling someone that supper was going on now.

Then it must be twelve o'clock.

Frederica approached Monica.

"We can dance now," she said eagerly. "Is your card full?"

"Quite full, thank you."

"Who is taking you down to supper?"

"A man who came to dinner with us. I can't remember his name."

"Our dance, I think, Miss Ingram."

It was Claude Ashe.

Monica looked at her mother, received a smiling nod of dismissal, and went off into the crowded ball-room. There

44

was very little room for dancing, but she and Claude Ashe revolved as briskly as was possible.

Monica enjoyed dancing, and the swift motion was a relief after standing so long.

She and her partner did not speak, at first, and Monica had leisure to look at her own reflection in the long glasses on the walls. She saw that she was wearing too serious an expression. Both her mother and the dancing-mistress had warned her about this, and she immediately assumed an air of fresh, sparkling enjoyment.

Once or twice she passed Frederica, dancing solemnly with Mr. Pelham. Monica could not remember having seen him arrive, but they exchanged bows and a smile. She wondered whether he would ask her to dance later. She had nothing left, excepting one of the "extras."

With a little shock of compassion she saw Cecily Marlowe —a wall-flower—sitting at the end of a row of chaperons, her face blank, her eyes and mouth listless.

Monica quickly looked away from her.

How *awful* to have to sit like that—so that everybody knew one wasn't being a success! Monica, gracefully twirling round and round with her partner, realized that the same thing might happen to herself at any time; but at least, she thought, if it did, she would pretend that she didn't mind a bit—would laugh and talk to the chaperons, so that perhaps people would think: What a nice, kind-hearted girl! She's ready to give up a dance for the sake of being attentive to her mother's friends!

"Are you enjoying your first ball?" Ashe asked her.

"Oh yes." Monica threw additional vivacity into her manner and expression. Her mother had often told her that men liked a girl to seem bright and happy, and to enjoy things.

"I expect you love dancing, don't you? You waltz most awfully well, if I may say so."

"Oh, I don't think I do it a *bit* well. I really don't."

"Yes, you do."

The waltz, to Monica's regret, came to an end.

Mr. Ashe took her to a corner, where two small armchairs stood beneath a potted palm.

"Shall I get you an ice or anything?"

"No, thank you, really, I shall be going down to supper next dance."

Monica felt that it might be as well to let him know that. It was always very important to be booked for supper. If a man asked if he might take one in to supper it meant that he really did want to talk to one.

These considerations did not formulate themselves very clearly in Monica's consciousness: they were simply amongst the things that she knew and accepted.

Ashe began to talk to her about South Wales, where his home was. It transpired that he liked sketching, and botany. He was rather apologetic about the latter taste, but said, as though in extenuation, that he had been allowed to make a hobby of it at Eton.

Monica said that she thought botany must be very interesting.

Had she, Claude Ashe wanted to know, ever been to Kew Gardens?

Monica never had. She immediately added that she had always *wanted* to go there.

What a triumph if this young man, whom she had only met to-night for the first time, were to suggest taking her there! Something would have to be arranged in the way of chaperonage, of course, but Monica knew that that would all be done for her.

She looked expectantly at him, then hastily looked away again. It never answered to let them see one was interested.

"I hope," said Mr. Ashe, in a slightly husky voice, "that perhaps one of these days, if you're not too busy, you'll let me arrange a little party, and go down there. I'm supposed to be eating my dinners in the Temple just now, but I've got plenty of time on my hands—Saturday afternoons, and all that, you know."

"I'd love to," said Monica prettily.

She hoped that he would suggest a date, and make the invitation definite, for she could not help feeling that it would establish her at once as a success if she could only tell her mother that the young man who had sat next to her at dinner wanted to meet her again.

But at that moment the first bars of the next dance sounded. The atmosphere changed: there was a general movement all round them, and after moment they both stood up.

"Would you like to find Mrs. Ingram?" said Ashe rather uncertainly.

"Well—I expect my next partner is looking for me," Monica replied, anxious to let him know that she was in demand.

"Oh, of course."

"Miss Ingram, may I have the pleasure of a dance with you?" It was Mr. Pelham, and as Monica turned towards him Claude Ashe bowed, and went away.

Later on in the evening he asked her for another dance, but she had none left. Monica was disappointed, but felt that it might be all for the best. As her mother always said, it made a man *much* keener if he didn't see quite as much of a girl as he wanted to. If things were made too easy for them, they lost interest.

Once or twice as she was dancing, Monica caught sight of Mr. Ashe, also dancing. He was so tall that it was easy to distinguish him, even before the ball-room began to grow empty. Once they exchanged a smile.

"Well, my darling, enjoying yourself?" Mrs. Ingram asked fondly, as her child paused for a moment beside her.

"Yes, thank you, I'm having a lovely time," Monica replied fervently. She would have said that in any case, but in actual fact the fervour was quite real. She was enjoying herself very much indeed.

"Don't get too hot, darling—and hold yourself up."

"Yes, mother."

"Have you been down to supper yet?"

"Oh yes."

"I hope you ate a proper meal. It's silly to think you can dance all night without anything to keep you going. Girls are so foolish," said Mrs. Ingram, turning in smiling appeal to the nearest chaperon.

"Oh, very foolish indeed."

Monica was well accustomed to hearing it said that the young were foolish. She knew that such was the opinion of her parents and of all their contemporaries, and she vaguely looked forward to the day when she should have left youth behind and become superior and experienced and infallible, herself.

None of her other partners proved quite as interesting as Claude Ashe had been, and there was a certain sameness about their conversation.

The theatres, the band, the floor, the dances that she was going to—did she know the Marlowe girls well?

To all of these questions, Monica returned the expected replies. To the enquiry about the Marlowes she carefully answered that they were both great friends of hers. The imprudence of ever saying anything derogatory about anybody had always been impressed upon Monica. If she could find nothing pleasant to say about a person, then it was wiser to keep silence altogether. One never knew that one's words might not be repeated.

So Monica proclaimed her friendship with Frederica and Cecily.

Towards the end of the evening she exchanged a few words with Cecily, standing waiting for the last dance on the programme to begin.

"Nearly everyone's going now. I think it's been a great success, don't you?"

"Oh yes," said Cecily listlessly.

"Are you tired?"

"No, not a bit, thanks," hastily answered Cecily, flushing and straightening herself.

Monica remembered that Cecily, living under the daily

48

and hourly tyranny of Frederica's morbid solicitude, never could endure a personal question, especially with reference to her own well-being. Vaguely it crossed her mind that intercourse with the Marlowes was terribly hampered by intangible restrictions and mysterious under-currents, and that it was no wonder they both seemed unhappy. . . . Almost directly a glow of satisfaction in her own greater freedom of mind took the place of her compassionate impulse.

"I'm not a bit tired either," she said brightly. "But one of my shoes is hurting like anything. I knew it would. I had it off during dinner, but I thought I was never going to get it on again in time."

"How awful!"

"Yes, wasn't it? Who are you dancing the last dance with, Cecily?"

"Mr. Pelham."

How dull, thought Monica. She herself was rather disappointed that Mr. Ashe had not asked her for the last dance. He had, in fact, gone away without saying good-bye to her, although she had seen him making a polite farewell speech to her mother.

The band broke into a galop, and Monica's partner—rather an uninteresting young man whose name she had not heard when he was introduced—claimed her.

"Straight home to bed after this, my darling," she heard her mother murmur as she went past.

Mrs. Ingram was sitting on a gilt chair near the door, every now and then obliged to jump up in order to receive the thanks and good-nights of departing guests.

The room was nearly empty.

Cecily Marlowe, trailing, rather than dancing, drooped over Mr. Pelham's shoulder. He was shorter by an inch or so than she was.

Frederica was standing beside her mother. Evidently no one had asked her for the last dance.

Suddenly the band broke into quick time. Monica's partner dashed with her across the room—then down, then up again—It was exhilarating, in spite of the agony of her pinched toes.

Breathless, they stopped when the music stopped.

It was all over.

"Good-night—it's been *too* delightful."

"Good-night, dear Mrs. Ingram—thank you for such a delightful evening. My girl has loved every minute of it."

One woman, in a black velvet dress that Monica thought much too *décolletée*, said to Mrs. Ingram:

"Such a success, Imogen darling! I've heard *everyone* saying how sweet your girl is."

Monica blushed and looked away.

"Now, my pet——" Mrs. Ingram hurried her daughter to the nearly empty cloak-room, and redeemed their wraps.

"Mother, I never said good-night to Lady Marlowe!"

"Never mind, I said it for you. She's probably half-way home by now. I must say it's hard on her that those two girls are so heavy in hand. They've had every chance—and yet look at them!"

"I think they danced most of the evening," Monica could afford to say, with conscious superiority.

"I should hope so, at their mother's ball! Though I saw both of them sitting out once or twice. Let it be a lesson to you, darling, *never* to let yourself seem bored and tired and listless. Nothing puts men off more quickly. Well, did you have a lovely time?"

"Oh, lovely, mother. I did enjoy it."

"That's right, darling. Now—into bed as quickly as possible. Parsons is sitting up—she can undo you first, before she comes down to me. And let her take down your hair and brush it out *thoroughly*, Monica. Otherwise it'll be all tangles to-morrow."

"I'm not really a bit sleepy, mother. Couldn't Parsons do you first?"

"No, darling. You heard what mother said. You're to sleep as late as you can in the morning, and ring for your breakfast to be brought up to you."

Monica had known that there would be no escaping this. She did not argue, aware that it would be useless, and feeling also the burden of obligation laid upon her by her mother, who had taken so much trouble and spent so much money in order that Monica might have a really good start, and meet as many young men as possible.

At the foot of the stairs, just before going up to bed, she kissed her parents and made them a rather embarrassed little speech, thanking them, and saying how much she had enjoyed herself.

Her mother answered as she always did, "I don't want any thanks, my child. Run along now."

Her father, more graciously, said:

"That's right, my dear little girl. I'm sure you'll show your gratitude by being very good and obedient and cheerful."

Monica said, "Yes, father," and went upstairs, stopping, directly she was out of sight, to take off her tight shoes.

She was actually in bed in the dark, before she remembered, with a slight pang, that no one, after all, had proposed to her at her first ball.

CHAPTER IV

THE SEASON continued.

Monica, now launched, was taken to balls, to dinner-parties and theatre-parties, to Hurlingham to watch the polo on Saturdays, and to the Days of all her mother's friends.

Twice her mother gave a girls' luncheon-party, explaining that this was very important and necessary, since it was by making friends with other girls that Monica would receive invitations to pay country-house visits.

"A girl gets far more chances in one house-party than at a dozen London balls," declared Mrs. Ingram.

Monica, of course, understood what her mother meant.

The luncheon-parties, with Mrs. Ingram at the head of the table—talking very brightly and carefully and not at all naturally—and herself at the foot, were not very amusing, but they led to her being asked to various tea-parties, and even to an occasional matinée.

Monica's mother was, comparatively, liberal-minded. She allowed her child to go out to matinées with only another girl, and to walk in the streets of Belgravia—*not* the Pimlico end and *not* beyond Harvey Nicholls at the top of Sloane Street—escorted only by a maid. Monica might go in cabs, even hansoms, although not in omnibuses, and she might travel alone by train, first-class, if her mother's maid went in the carriage with her.

Frederica and Cecily Marlowe, especially Frederica, envied Monica her emancipation.

They had no freedom at all.

Monica still saw more of the Marlowes than of anybody else, and because of the old schoolroom intimacy, felt more at home with them than with girls nearer to her own age.

She was fond of Cecily, and sorry for her, although contemptuous of her supineness and of her terrified evasions of personal contacts. Frederica, Monica did not really like at all, but she had a kind of unwilling admiration for a force of character that she felt, rather than understood, whilst at the same time she experienced a definite gratification, of which she was slightly ashamed, because she knew that Frederica was unpopular with men.

It would, indeed, have been impossible not to know this, for Lady Marlowe had taken up the line of jesting about it openly. She was half-Italian, and had a reputation for caustic wit. It was generally recognized that her daughters were a disappointment to her. Like almost every woman of her generation, she had wished to have sons, and regarded the sex of her two girls as being something between a disgrace and a calamity—and it was felt that she showed at least courage and originality, even if indifferent taste, in jeering, lightly and amusingly, at their failure to attract.

"If Frederica hasn't succeeded in finding a husband by the time she's twenty-five, I shall give her what she'd have had if she'd married and let her go and live where she likes and do what she likes," declared Lady Marlowe, laughing merrily. "Why not? It's ruining any chances Cecily may have, for men to see Fricky trailing about the place, with never even a nibble."

She had given up the fiction, once offered to her friends, that Frederica, once at least, could have married. She now shrugged her shoulders and said instead that it was very odd she should have unattractive daughters.

So indeed it was, for Lady Marlowe, already twice widowed, could very easily have married again had she chosen to do so. Men liked her, and were amused by her.

When she gave small dinner-parties, they wanted to talk to her, and listen to her—not to either of the girls. Even at balls she attracted far more attention, with her sparkle and vitality, than did her two joyless, drooping daughters, trailing silently in her wake.

"Can't you be natural and bright?" Lady Marlowe sometimes despairingly, and yet half humorously, enquired of Frederica. But Frederica continued to be neither natural nor bright. It was she who sometimes revolted against their mother. Cecily never did. But it was part of Cecily's misery that Frederica's revolts were, so often, on her behalf.

For Frederica's warped and thwarted individuality had thrown out a strange, one-sided growth in the form of a violently protective and possessive solicitude for her sister.

"Have you got a headache?"

She could never let Cecily alone.

"Are you tired?"

"You won't care for that book, Cecily. Have this one instead."

She could not even bear to let Cecily read a novel that might bring her into vicarious contact with life. It might mean that she would be hurt. It might mean that she would escape, or wish to escape, from Frederica's domination.

Frederica, at twenty-four, would manœuvre elaborately to keep the newspaper out of Cecily's view, because she did not like her to read it. She wanted Cecily to remain a child. Cecily had once, under the pressure of Lady Marlowe's mockery and of Frederica's imperative cross-questionings, admitted that she did think that, really, women ought to have the vote.

"You can't really think that. You don't know enough about it," Frederica declared, instantly terrified by vague and irrational previsions of Cecily wanting to join the movement, falling under strange influences, perhaps being sent to prison.

And Lady Marlowe, with her clear, unkind laugh, told Cecily not to be a silly little goose.

"These women who are making a fuss about getting a vote are simply hysterical old maids, or women who can't get on with their husbands. They only want to make themselves conspicuous. As if any woman who knew her job couldn't influence at least *one* man to vote the way she wants him to!"

Then she looked at the two dreary young faces staring back at hers—Frederica's tense and sullen with suppressed rebellion, and Cecily's secret and withdrawn, and shrugged her shoulders.

"I only wish you had a man to influence, my poor child. If one of you doesn't get married soon, I really think you'd better go into a convent, both of you. Though even then, people would only say it was because you couldn't find anyone to marry you."

Frederica, goaded beyond endurance, suddenly exclaimed:

"I don't want to get married. I hate men. I wouldn't marry anyone—whoever it was."

Lady Marlowe gazed at her in astonishment for a moment, and then laughed again.

"So you've got to that stage, have you?" was all she said.

Frederica, turning aside—she would not have dared to leave the room without an excuse, and was unable to speak —sank her teeth into the soft flesh of her thin wrist until tiny purple marks sprang into view.

Lady Marlowe, although she often said cruel things, was not a cruel woman, but only an almost entirely unfeeling one.

By some curious effort on the part of Nature to redress the balance, she had attracted to herself in the person of her second husband a gentle, serious-minded, and intensely sensitive man, many years older than herself, who had mistaken her liveliness for mirth, her hardness for courage, and her coarseness of fibre for a protective armour, donned to conceal a passionate spirit that should reveal itself to his tenderness. He was himself wholly vulnerable where his affections were concerned, and without the resilience of youth.

Very soon after his marriage he allowed his natural lethargy—from which the timid dawnings of a belated love had temporarily roused him—to take possession of him altogether.

Although he was a man to whom physical relations with a woman whom he no longer loved imaginatively soon became entirely repugnant, he felt sure that it was his duty to beget children. Moreover, he lacked the moral courage to risk offending his wife.

First Frederica, and then Cecily, were brought into the world, to inherit a quadrupled share of their father's timidity, his fastidiousness, his morbid unwillingness to face unpleasant facts, his eager desire for affection, and his utter inability to compel it.

He, like his wife, felt slightly ashamed that both the children should be girls, and during their early childhood he found the physical side of their existence, so inevitably stressed in nursery days, unpleasantly obtrusive.

Just before Cecily's sixth birthday her father fell ill with influenza. He was not very ill—nevertheless he died. He left everything to his wife—his money, the house in Belgrave Square, and the place in Yorkshire. There was no mention of his children in the will since neither was a boy.

Lady Marlowe let the place in Yorkshire and lived in the Belgrave Square house. Frederica and Cecily had a French mademoiselle, who taught them to speak and write French, and with whom they read and reread the stories of Mme. de Ségur and Mlle. Zenaïde Fleuriot, because Mademoiselle said that nothing else was proper for young girls—and a children's maid, who brushed their hair, bathed them, and dressed and undressed them, exactly as she had done in their childhood, until both were well on in their teens.

Their mother's authority was supreme. No one in the house was allowed to question it, but Frederica and Cecily least of all. If Frederica sometimes, in what her mother referred to as "the difficult age," made occasional clumsy and defiant attempts at self-assertion, they were met with such open ridicule that she could not persist in them. She was both too hyper-sensitive and too ill-adjusted to find any means of retaliation. Her violent and unformulated resentment of her mother's tyranny reacted upon Cecily, who had thus a double yoke to bear: that of Lady Marlowe's cheerful bullying, and that of Frederica's morbid and possessive love.

Cecily was, however, the less unhappy of the two. The vitality that in Frederica was suppressed and distorted, in Cecily was reduced to a minimum, so that her life was almost entirely mental. Where Frederica yearned fiercely for normal contacts with humanity and life, Cecily longed for the education that had been almost wholly denied to her, and sought refuge from all that was unendurable in her life in abstract speculation and pathetic, surreptitious delvings into such sources of learning as she could attain to in secret.

Both girls bore an immense and unacknowledged sense of guilt always with them, since both practised continual deceptions, ranging from direct lies to subtle reservations and implications, in regard to one another and to their parent. They were never, indeed, frank with anyone—Cecily because she unconsciously sought to safeguard herself against life by avoiding personal contacts, and Frederica because bitterness so distorted her vision that she could scarcely distinguish the false from the true.

They had never been friendly with other girls, but Mrs. Ingram's gentle insistence in forcing Monica upon them had led to a certain degree of familiarity between the three.

They talked more or less freely, in the Belgrave Square schoolroom or in the back half of Mrs. Ingram's drawing-room, which Monica was allowed to use as a sitting-room in the mornings.

Towards the end of Monica's first season she began, almost imperceptibly, to adopt an air of faint superiority towards Frederica. Not towards Cecily, for Cecily was too meek to provoke one to superiority. She would have taken the superiority of almost anybody for granted.

"Fancy, that Mr. Pelham that I met here, asks me to dance at every single ball I see him at. I danced with him twice on Tuesday, at the Corrys'."

"He's very dull though, isn't he?" said Frederica.

"Oh, I don't think so. Of course he's rather old, but I don't mind that a bit. I rather like elderly men; they're easier to talk to, I think."

"Mr. Pelham is supposed to have proposed to five different girls, and they all refused him. He's dying to find a wife."

"Is he? I should have thought he'd be miles better than no one," said Monica, surprised. "He's quite rich, isn't he?"

"I think so. But deadly. I've practically given up dancing with him," said Frederica, looking straight at Monica.

She, too, had been at the Corrys' ball, and Monica had seen her, with a white, stiffening face, sitting out dance after dance.

"Why?"

"I just don't care about dancing, except with my particular friends. I'd really rather sit and watch."

Monica felt something that was half-way between pity for Frederica and anger at having it supposed that she would be stupid enough to believe such nonsense.

Cecily interposed.

"Monica, did you go to Kew Gardens with the Ashes?"

"Yes, on Saturday. Alice Ashe arranged a party. It was rather fun."

"Was Claude there?"

They always spoke of all the young men whom they knew by their Christian names, and scrupulously addressed them as Mr.

"Of course he was," said Frederica, laughing. "Monica thinks that he arranged the whole thing for her."

"As a matter of fact, he did. He practically said so. Considering he was the only person there I really knew—he'd introduced me and his sister, Alice, the day before, so that she could invite me."

"I think he looks very nice," said Cecily.

"He's quite nice," Monica threw out, with elaborate casualness.

"Boys are no use except to play about with, though."

"He's twenty-six."

"Is he? Oh well, that's different. I didn't realize he was as old as that," said Frederica, more respectfully.

"Would he be any good, Monica?" Cecily enquired wistfully.

They all knew what she meant. A man was "any good" or "no good" according to whether he could, or could not, ask one to marry him.

"I don't know. I don't suppose he has any money. His people don't sound at all rich, from what Alice Ashe said about their house. They live somewhere in Wales."

"And he's a barrister, or something. Like Mr. Pelham."

"Yes. That would mean living in London if——"

"Would you mind that?"

"Oh no. One can always pay visits," said Monica cheerfully.

"It would be awfully exciting if one of us got engaged," said Cecily.

"Yes, wouldn't it. The other two would have to be bridesmaids, of course."

"How, exactly, would you have your bridesmaids dressed, and what colour would you choose for your going-away frock?" said Frederica thoughtfully. "Let's all say in turns."

It was an imaginative exercise of which they were never tired—discussing the details of a wedding, each one visualizing herself as its central figure. Even Mrs. Ingram, Monica's mother, would sometimes indulge in the same pastime, alone with her daughter.

It was not very long before Claude Ashe, calling on Mrs. Ingram only a very few days after the expedition to Kew, was smilingly told to go and find Monica in the back drawing-room. Monica, pleased, but rather nervous, jumped up. As she came forward through the looped-back blue satin curtains that divided the big room, she saw, behind Claude Ashe, her mother's quick frown and shake of the head.

She guessed that she had shown too much eagerness in her rapid movement to greet the young man, and felt more self-conscious than ever. However after a few moments it wore off, and she was talking almost naturally about the little drawings that strewed the table.

They were bad little drawings, copied, as Monica had been taught to copy, from picture-books, or Christmas cards, or an occasional magazine illustration. Children in Dutch peasant costumes, thatched cottages crouching behind rampant herbaceous borders—even ducks, carrying umbrellas, or emerging from improbable-looking eggs.

These copies, carefully and brightly painted with water-colour paint by Monica, adorned her mother's menu-cards.

"I don't mean her to be *idle*, just because she's 'out,' " Mrs. Ingram always said. "At least one hour at some little job, every day, is one of my rules."

"I say, did you do those? How awfully clever of you," cried Mr. Ashe. He was most appreciative and Monica felt, with complete satisfaction, that it wasn't really the painting he was admiring—he said at once that he knew nothing whatever about Art—but herself.

They were talking very happily—from Art they had passed on to politics, and Monica had admitted that she often felt inclined to read up Socialism, although it would shock her parents most *dreadfully* if they ever guessed it—when Mrs. Ingram summoned Monica to the other room.

"You must tell me some more another time," said Claude Ashe earnestly, as he rose to his feet.

"I expect I've been boring you most frightfully, really," Monica murmured insincerely.

"I've simply loved it. You know I have. I only hope *you* haven't been bored."

"Oh no. I've loved it too."

Avoiding the young man's eye, and blushing a good deal, Monica preceded him into the further room.

There were several other callers there now, and she had no more conversation with Claude, although she was all the time acutely aware of his presence in the room. She could tell by the quick way her mother looked at her, and then away again, that she was eager to know exactly how the *tête-à-tête* had progressed.

Sure enough, as soon as the last visitor had gone—Claude went away quite soon, and at a moment when Monica, helping an elderly lady on with her feather boa, could only smile and bow—Mrs. Ingram turned to her daughter.

"How did you and young Ashe get on, darling?"

"Quite nicely, thank you, mother."

"I couldn't leave you chatting alone with him in the back drawing-room any longer. It would have been much too marked."

"Yes, of course."

"Besides——"

Mrs. Ingram paused so long that Monica, rather anxiously, ventured to ask:

"Besides what, mother?"

"Besides, though he may be a very nice young man, we've got to remember that he isn't, really, very much use. He's too young, for one thing, and there's no money at all, even if he hadn't got an elder brother."

Monica, disconcerted and disappointed, did not quite know how to reply. She was afraid that her mother was going to say that she would not be allowed to be friends with Claude Ashe any more.

"It's quite all right, darling," said Mrs. Ingram very kindly. "I like you to make friends of your own age, and one wants people to see that—well, that there's someone running after you, more or less. Only I want you to realize that you mustn't take anything at all seriously, just yet."

"Oh, I won't, mother," said Monica, quite relieved.

"It's only your first season, after all, and you're very young. Though I wasn't much older than you are now when I married."

Monica had very often been told that Mrs. Ingram had married at eighteen, and the information always vaguely annoyed her.

"I suppose you must have been very pretty when you

were young," she said politely, trying not to know too consciously that she was saying something very nasty indeed.

Imogen Ingram laughed curtly.

She was not yet forty, and although her complexion had faded, her hair, eyes, and teeth were still beautiful. It was, of course, natural and suitable that she should display ample curves both above and below her tightly corseted waist. Men always preferred a full figure to a skinny one.

"You're a little goose, Monica," she said kindly. "I had the freshness of youth, of course, as a girl, but I don't suppose otherwise I've altered so very much. And prettiness isn't really very important, darling. A great many very pretty girls never get a chance of marrying at all, and some quite plain ones turn out attractive to men. One never can tell. Father always said that he first fell in love with me because he thought I was natural, and unaffected, and didn't think about myself all the time. No really nice man ever cares about a girl who's affected, or self-conscious."

Monica hoped ardently that she was neither of these things.

Claude Ashe, at all events, did not think so. She was sure that he liked her very much. Perhaps, even, he was falling in love with her. If he was, would he say so—and when?

The season was nearly over, and Monica and her parents were to pay two country-house visits, spend a month in Scotland, and after that, said Mrs. Ingram, Monica could go to the Marlowes—Lady Marlowe was taking a furnished house near Oxford for the whole of September—whilst her parents went to join a large house-party where Royalty was to be met.

"I wish you'd been asked too, my pet," said Mrs. Ingram, "but naturally people don't want young girls about. It limits conversation, and everything. When you're married, it'll be quite different."

Girlhood was indeed, Monica felt, an inferior state from which escape was desirable at any cost.

What a pity that one couldn't accept Claude Ashe, even

if he did propose! Probably, however, he never would, for no really nice and honourable man proposed to a girl unless he was in a position to offer her a home at least as comfortable as the one from which he was taking her.

A week before she was to leave London, Monica was invited by Lady Margaret Miller to dine, and go with a large party of young people—chaperoned by Lady Margaret's married daughter—to the White City.

"Yes, of course you may go," said Mrs. Ingram. "I certainly shouldn't allow you to go to dinner-parties without me in the ordinary way, but an old friend like Lady Margaret is different. It's very kind of her indeed. Write a nice little note and accept, Monica. You'd better let me see it."

Monica did not like her mother's spasmodic supervision of her correspondence, but there was no escaping from it. As though, she thought, she did not know all the rules about letter-writing, that had been impressed upon her ever since she could write at all!

"Never begin a letter with 'I'——"

"Put '*My* dear So-and-so' to a person older or more important than yourself."

"Always read through a letter before closing it, and if anything has been left out, rewrite the letter—don't add it in."

"Never put a P.S. It's vulgar."

Avoiding these and other pitfalls, Monica wrote her acceptance to Lady Margaret.

Next evening, a telephone message came from her kind hostess. A young man had failed, for the White City party—was there anybody whom Monica would specially like asked, whom Lady Margaret could invite in place of the defaulter?

The Ingrams were finishing dinner when Mrs. Ingram was called to the telephone, and Monica could hear, from the little room next door, her own name and her mother's proper expressions of gratitude and assurances that it really was *much* too kind.

Presently Mrs. Ingram returned and explained.

"Oh, really, that's *too* good of her," said Vernon Ingram. "I never heard of anything so kind. Monica, do you understand that Lady Margaret is good enough to be suggesting that you should submit to her the name of some young man whom you'd like her to invite to her house?"

Monica felt embarrassed by her father's excessive sense of the privilege conferred upon her.

"Well, really," said Mrs. Ingram, "I don't quite know what to do. I told Lady Margaret I'd telephone to her the first thing to-morrow morning. Of course Monica must write a note as well. Now, we must think——"

Monica had thought already, but she knew better than to say so.

The butler placed the dessert dishes on the table, and approached Mr. Ingram with the port decanter.

Neither Mrs. Ingram nor Monica ever drank any, and they watched Palter's measured progress with impatience.

The moment the door had shut behind him, Monica's mother spoke.

"It must be someone we know fairly well, otherwise it becomes rather too marked. What about Claude Ashe, darling?"

Monica nearly jumped.

She looked at her mother, but there was no sign of any special significance to be seen.

"I think he'd do very well," she replied carefully.

"Well, then, you'd better ring him up to-morrow—or, wait a minute; I think it would come better from me, perhaps. *I'll* ring him up."

"A very good idea," said Vernon Ingram approvingly. "A nice young fellow, and not at all likely to think any young lady is running after him."

He laughed a little as he spoke.

"Why, father?"

"Why, my dear child? Because I hope he's a modest young man, and because, as he's not in a position to marry at all, at present, he can't suppose that he is being pursued with that end in view."

64

Vernon Ingram pushed back his chair from the table.

"It's quite pleasant to have a quiet evening at home together, once in a while," he remarked, as he opened the door for his wife and daughter.

They left him, as usual, for his customary quarter of an hour in the dining-room, whilst they sat in the drawing-room.

Mrs. Ingram picked up the newspaper, and Monica went to the piano. She would not have been encouraged to read the newspaper, even had she wished to do so, and it would have been bad manners to read a book unless her mother had also been doing the same.

So she opened "The Star Folio" and played Beethoven's *Adieux* and a waltz, *Sobre les Olas*.

"That will do now, darling," said Mrs. Ingram. "I can hear father coming, and he may want to talk. Ring for coffee."

Monica obeyed.

She was not really particularly interested in either the *Adieux* or *Sobre les Olas*, although she vaguely liked the idea of herself, in a simple white frock, dreamily playing under the lamplight, and it always rather annoyed her that her conception of her own appearance had to be spoilt by the fact that, having no faculty for playing by ear, she was obliged always to keep her eyes fixed upon her music.

All the time she had been playing she had been thinking about Claude Ashe. It made a person much more interesting and exciting, somehow, if you thought about him to the sound of music.

Neither of her parents mentioned Ashe again. The evening, to Monica's dismay, was spent in trying to learn Bridge. Her father was teaching her mother as well as herself. Mrs. Ingram got on fairly well—she had played whist for many years—but Monica, as usual, forgot what were trumps, mixed clubs with spades, and persistently failed to return her partner's lead.

At ten o'clock she went up to bed in tears.

CHAPTER V

"MISS MARY COLLIER—Miss Monica Ingram—Mr. David Collier—Miss Monica Ingram—Captain Christopher Lane—Miss Collier, Miss Ingram. There—I think you all know each other now. Oh—I'm sorry—Mr. Ashe, Captain Lane—You know Miss Ingram, of course?"

Mr. Ashe bowed, and Monica smiled.

She was enjoying herself already, although she had only just arrived at Lady Margaret's house in South Audley Street. All the guests were young, even the chaperon of the party, Lady Margaret's married daughter, and her husband.

"It was most awfully nice of you and your mother to suggest my being asked," said Claude Ashe, in a low voice.

"I'm so glad you were able to come," rejoined Monica. She was thinking how tactful it had been of him to include her mother in his gratitude. Like that, it didn't look as if he thought that Monica had—odious phrase!—been running after him.

They were to have dinner at the Exhibition.

"Let me see——"

Lady Margaret—kind, short-sighted, and incurably match-making—was peering at her youthful friends, only anxious to please them all, and to make sure that those who wanted to be together should be together.

"Mary, supposing you and Joan"—Joan was Lady Margaret's unmarried daughter—" go with David and—let me see—Ronald in his car. And, Captain Lane, will you take care of my daughter Dorothy, if you don't mind a taxi-cab? Now, what about you, Monica? Will you and Mr. Ashe go in the carriage with Peter and Rachel? I dare say it'll get there just as soon as they will, in their machines."

66

It was quite certain that it would do nothing of the kind, and everyone laughed politely at Lady Margaret's little joke. Everyone also agreed—naturally—to her suggestions.

Monica looked at the other girls.

Rachel Modbury's engagement to Peter Miller had just been announced, and Monica gazed at her eagerly. She was not pretty, but had a fresh, cheerful face, with a slightly open mouth, no chin, and candid-looking hazel eyes. Every time that Peter spoke to her she giggled. On the fourth finger of her left hand was an enormous emerald. Monica did not care for her dress—a fussy affair of pink tulle, with a broad pink scarf, matching the pink *bandeau* that was bound round her fuzzy fair hair.

Joan Miller, who was much prettier, wasn't engaged to anybody, and she must be older than the Rachel girl. Monica wondered whether she minded.

The girl who had been introduced as Mary Collier, Monica had never seen before. She was very tall and dark, with a slightly underhung jaw, and straight black eyebrows over a pair of deep grey eyes. She wore a very plain satin dress, of an unusual shade of green, and her thick black hair was parted in the middle, and had not been fluffed out at all. Monica decided that she *certainly* wasn't pretty, although she might be called interesting-looking.

It really did seem, although one hardly liked even to think such a thing, as if she herself were the prettiest girl there. Monica could not help wondering if anybody else thought so too.

She had on a new frock, that her mother had said was exactly right for this kind of occasion. Not too much of an evening-dress, yet with a charming little V-neck, of very palest blue satin, covered with blue net, and with a little bunch of forget-me-nots at the waist.

Did Claude Ashe think her pretty? However many times Monica reminded herself, and was reminded, of her mother's axiom, that prettiness was *not* the thing that counted most, she still wanted Claude Ashe to think her pretty. She felt

67

self-conscious whenever she caught his eye, and looked resolutely away from him and at the other men.

Peter Miller was not in the least interesting since he was now engaged to be married; but David Collier might be nice—tall and dark, like his sister, but younger-looking. The remaining man (Lady Margaret's son-in-law—like Peter—did not count) was Captain Lane, and Monica had neither met him nor heard of him before.

She was, without quite knowing it, at once prepared to like him because he was very big—a tall young man, heavily built, and with fair hair already receding from his temples at twenty-nine—and had a deep, loud, masculine voice, and a habit of staring down into the eyes of any woman with whom he shook hands.

The drive was most amusing. It was the first time that Monica had been allowed to go anywhere, unchaperoned, with young men and girls of her own age, all of whom knew one another and one another's world, and in whose free-masonry she felt herself to be immediately included. She found herself talking and laughing quite naturally even with Claude Ashe—presently, indeed, it was especially with Claude Ashe.

Although he was so quiet he could say amusing things, gently and unexpectedly, and Monica noticed with a thrill of pleasure that it was her eyes that he sought with his own, when they all laughed together.

The party had arranged to meet at the entrance and to have dinner on arrival. Monica wondered if Claude Ashe would take the chair next to hers at dinner. Surely, surely, if he *did*, that would almost amount to a proof.

"Ladies and gentlemen, sort yourselves, as the parson said at the double wedding," cried Dorothy humorously, and they all laughed again.

"May I come here?" said Claude, and he put his hand on the chair next to Monica's.

She felt more and more excited and happy as the gay, noisy dinner went on. Dorothy's husband had ordered cham-

68

pagne, and although Monica, who still hated the unaccustomed taste, only sipped at hers, she felt that her face was becoming flushed, and her voice and her laughter much readier than usual.

On her other side sat Captain Lane, and presently he was rallying her about her bunch of forget-me-nots, as though they had known one another for years.

"When are you going to stop talking to that fellow, and talk to me instead?" Claude murmured jealously.

Monica was intoxicated with success.

After dinner, they all wandered about together for a little while, then gradually drifted to the Amusements.

"Let's go on the switchback."

"The water-chute is ripping."

"Oh yes, do let's go on the water-chute!"

It was Claude who helped Monica into the boat, and sat next to her. She was aware of his presence, even in the tense excitement of approaching the steep slope down which the boat was to dash. . . .

"Oh—oh—I'm terrified. . . . Is it safe?"

"It's all right!"

They all screamed as the boat shot over the edge.

Monica, clutching the edge of the boat as it rocked madly into smoothness again, felt what a mercy it was that she had retained presence of mind enough not to grasp at her neighbour, which would have been embarrassing.

"Did you like it?"

"Oh, it was glorious!"

"Come on; let's go down again! They say it's more fun when you're used to it."

"Well, I shan't. I think it's simply awful," declared Joan Miller. "I'm going on the switchback. I'm sure it's a much more painless death."

Laughing with and at one another, they formed into small, separate parties. Monica, with Claude Ashe, Captain Lane, and Mary Collier, prepared to enjoy again the thrill of the water-chute.

This time she shared her small seat in the boat with Captain Lane. He took up a great deal more room than Claude Ashe had done, she could not help noticing.

A number of people had crowded in front of them—they were in the last seat of all, and Mary Collier and Claude Ashe, unable to get places at all, stood laughing and making signs that they would get into the next boat.

"We're off!"

"Hold tight!"

"Ow-ow!" The girl in front of Monica was screaming.

Monica did not scream. She caught her breath, and, half jubilant and half alarmed, turned to Captain Lane.

He smiled down at her—an attractive smile, revealing admirable teeth; and at the same instant the boatman called out a warning: "Off she goes!"

Monica gasped involuntarily.

At almost the same instant she felt Lane's arm round her waist, and, as the boat shot over the waterfall, he caught her closely to him.

Sensations as unfamiliar as they were exciting rushed upon Monica.

In one bewildering moment she felt profoundly shocked and unspeakably elated.

The boat rocked. . . . Lane relaxed his hold, shifted his arm slightly, and, holding Monica by the shoulder, gently forced her to look round at him.

"Wasn't that wonderful?"

Monica had not the least idea what she ought to say. Instinctively, she referred everything, as she had been taught to do from babyhood, to the bar of her mother's judgment, and she knew, of course, that her mother would say that Captain Lane was behaving like a cad, and that Monica must instantly make it clear to him that she was Not that Kind of Girl.

Monica, did not, however, know how to do this.

Worse still, she did not want to do it.

"Did you enjoy it?"

She pretended to think that he meant the waterfall.

"I wasn't as frightened as I was the first time."

He laughed.

"Where are the others?" said Monica hurriedly.

"I don't know—and, what's more, I don't think I very much care. Neither do you."

"But I do!" Monica said without conviction.

She could not resist looking up at him as she spoke, and he looked down into her eyes and laughed.

"I'm not going to let Ashe monopolize you as he did at dinner. It's my turn now—I've been waiting for it all the evening. Mind that step!"

He put his hand beneath her elbow, steadying her as she got out of the boat, and again that unfamiliar thrill went all through her.

"Have you been on the switchback yet?"

"No."

"Come on, then. We'll go."

He was being masterful, exactly like the people in books! Monica found it entrancing. She had never felt in the least like this with Claude Ashe, who was not masterful at all, and indeed, in a few minutes she had forgotten the very existence of Claude Ashe.

Christopher Lane was saying things in his deep, booming voice.

"I didn't think I was going to meet anyone like you this evening. Joan asked me, and she said the Colliers were coming and a Miss Ingram who was only just out, and I wasn't a bit interested. I don't like girls who are only just out."

"Never?"

"Well, hardly ever," Lane laughed.

Monica thought the repartee brilliant.

"*I'm* always frightened of people who are older than I am."

"Always?"

"Well, nearly always."

They laughed together. It was wonderful.

On the switchback Lane asked if she was nervous.

"Terrified," said Monica, not certain of what the answer might lead to, but knowing that was what he meant her to say.

"I'll hold your hand," he promptly declared.

His clasp was gentle, and yet strong and protective. Again, the feeling of being at once shocked and delighted went all through her, but this time pleasure and wild excitement predominated over every other sensation.

Down, and up again, flew the little trolley—Lane's large hand tightened upon Monica's and instinctively her fingers returned the pressure.

The car negotiated a sharp curve, and Monica, unresisting, was swung against his shoulder. When the end of the brief, nerve-racking transit was reached she was almost lying in his arms.

He released her instantly as the motion ceased, but kept her hand in his.

"Would you have liked that better with Ashe?"

Monica shook her head.

"Let's do it again, shall we?"

"I—I don't think so."

Christopher Lane immediately bought two more tickets for the next journey, for which the trolleys were already filling up again.

"Are you angry with me?"

Monica, feeling sure she ought to say Yes, but afraid that if she did he might believe her, and not like her any more, said nothing.

"You're not *really*, are you?"

His voice sounded dreadfully anxious.

She still remained silent, not looking at him.

"If you are," said Captain Christopher Lane—and his voice now was grave, and rather cold—"of course, I'll take you back to the others at once. Please do tell me, if you'd rather I did."

She had vexed him!

In a panic at the thought of such a thing, Monica looked up at him.

"But I wouldn't!"

"You—darling!"

She couldn't be certain of the word. It was lost in the noise going on all around them. But there was no mistaking the expression on his face.

"Stand back, please—cars all full up now——!"

They were off.

Monica longed ardently to feel her hand in his again. He made no movement. Incredibly—and surely involuntarily?— she looked round, although without moving. Instantly, as though at a signal, his hand closed over hers.

Bliss invaded her.

This, surely, was love—the most wonderful thing in life. Monica forgot to think about her mother, and what her mother would have thought and said of Captain Lane—forgot about the rest of the party—forgot about time itself.

After the switchback, they wandered about in the semi-darkness, still holding hands and talking. Christopher was no longer laughing and teasing her. He was talking to her quite seriously about himself, and telling her how much he wished that he could have met someone like her earlier in his life.

"We can be friends now, though," Monica assured him, earnestly and diffidently.

"Will you really?"

"If you really want me to."

"You know I do."

"Then I will. Of course I will. I—I'd love to."

"You're the most wonderful girl I've ever met! May I call you Monica?"

"Oh!"

She was thinking how shocked the Millers would be, who knew that she had met him for the first time that evening. They would probably speak of it to Lady Margaret, who in her turn might tell Monica's mother.

73

As though he had guessed her sudden panic, Christopher added: "Only when we're by ourselves—Monica. Because I want to see a great deal of you."

"Oh," she cried, "I wish we weren't going away! But we shall be leaving London next week, I'm afraid."

"Then we must meet as often as possible before you go. What are you doing to-morrow?"

"Hurlingham, in the afternoon."

"Good; that's easy."

"Shall you be there?" gasped Monica, hardly able to believe in such good fortune.

"Of course. If there's a chance of seeing you."

"I shall be with mother."

"Anybody else?"

"No one else is coming with us, but I expect we shall meet people we know."

"*One* person you know, anyhow," he said, looking into her eyes and smiling; and at the tingling sensation that ran through her veins like fire Monica forgot that for one anxious instant she had waited to hear him ask for an introduction to Mrs. Ingram.

"I'm horribly afraid that I ought to take you back to the others now—wherever they may be. It's getting rather late."

Monica was horrified that this reminder of the time should have come from him rather than from herself.

"I was just going to say that we ought to look for them," she lied hurriedly.

Christopher put his hand on her arm, drawing her further away from the lights.

"I want to say good-night to you first," he told her softly.

Although she did not exactly know what to expect, Monica's heart began to beat violently.

"Oughtn't we to hurry?"

"Not for a minute. I think you're perfectly sweet, Monica. The loveliest thing I've ever seen."

"Oh!"

"Do you like me a tiny bit?"

74

"You know I do," she whispered, nearly suffocated by the throbbing in her breast.

Could he be going to ask her to marry him?

Christopher put his hand under her chin, and gently tilted her face upwards.

"Good-night, you little darling."

He bent his head. Obeying a blind instinct, Monica turned her face sideways, so that his kiss alighted on the middle of her cheek.

For a moment the world stood still round her. . . .

"There they are!"

It was Joan Miller's voice.

"Is that you, Lane?"

"Where on earth have you been?" calmly enquired Christopher Lane. "We've been looking for you."

"And *we've* been looking for *you*. Is Mr. Ashe with you?"

"No. We left him at the water-chute," Lane explained, and his manner somehow made it seem as though he and Monica had left the water-chute but a moment ago.

"Oh, well, I expect we shall pick him up at the gate. We said we'd all meet there about eleven o'clock, if we got separated. Rachel wants to get home. Her mother said she wasn't to be late."

Scarcely knowing what she did, Monica walked on with the others. They were all there, excepting Claude Ashe.

Christopher Lane was no longer beside her. She could hear him talking to Joan.

"Hasn't it been fun?" said Rachel Modbury, in her flat, unenthusiastic voice that always had the same faintly pleasant inflections.

"Yes, perfectly glorious."

At the entrance they found a tall form standing rather aimlessly.

"Oh, there's Mr. Ashe. Good!" The young chaperon was evidently relieved at having collected all her party again.

"Now, how are we going home? The same way that we came?"

"No, Dorothy," said her sister. "We'd better divide up according to the directions we're going in—you know what I mean."

Discussion, and a certain amount of giggling, ensued. Rachel's mother had sent a car for her, and Peter insisted that he must see her safely home.

"Monica, you're Eaton Square, and the Colliers are Eaton Place—hadn't you better all go together?"

"We're taking a taxi," said Mary Collier. "Can't we give you a lift, Miss Ingram?"

"May I ask for one in the same direction?" Christopher enquired.

"Certainly."

"What about you, Mr. Ashe? Can we——?"

"I shall go by the District Railway," replied Mr. Ashe sepulchrally.

He was standing next to Monica.

"Good-night, and thank you most awfully for—for suggesting that I should come to-night."

Monica shook hands with him mechanically. His hand seemed extraordinarily limp as it held hers loosely for an instant and then let it drop. She returned the long look that he gave her quite unseeingly; and he turned away and said good-bye to the others without another word to Monica.

The drive back through the comparatively empty streets was a swift and rather silent one. Monica leaned back in her corner next to Mary Collier, feeling all at once more tired than ever in her life before.

Christopher Lane and David Collier sat opposite, and whenever the light of a street-lamp fell upon them Monica could see that Christopher was looking at her.

"Which comes first—you or us?" demanded Mary Collier.

"We'd better drop Miss Ingram first, I should think," her brother returned courteously.

At the Ingrams' door, both young men got out.

"Shall I ring?" asked Christopher. He was half-way to the bell already.

Monica had no latch key, but the taxi, driving into the quiet square, had evidently been heard, for a light appeared above the fanlight.

"It's all right."

She exchanged polite thanks and farewells with the Colliers.

"Good-night," said Christopher Lane, very low and quickly. He crushed her fingers tightly in his. "Good-night, Monica darling. Don't forget to-morrow, at Hurlingham."

"As if I could!" Monica answered under her breath. She released her hand and sprang forward, just as the door opened.

"Thank you, William," said Monica to the footman. She had been taught to reward servants for such extra services as sitting up at night by a smile and a few polite words, and she now saw with surprise that the clock in the hall showed it to be long past midnight.

"I hope you've had a pleasant evening, Miss."

"Yes, thank you. Very."

"Madam desired that you would go to her room at once on your return, Miss Monica."

"All right, William. Thank you. Good-night."

"Good-night, Miss Monica."

Monica had known that there would be no escaping the visit to her mother's bedroom—nor the glass of detested hot milk that she felt certain awaited her there.

She went slowly upstairs, leaving William to extinguish the light in the hall before retiring to the basement where he slept.

There was no light to be seen under her mother's door, but this did not release Monica from the obligation of knocking softly upon it.

"Come in."

Mrs. Ingram sat up in the big double bed and switched on the green-shaded bedside lamp as her daughter came in. To Monica, there was nothing strange, or even unfamiliar, in the astonishing difference between her mother up and dressed

77

and her mother in bed; for she was accustomed to the double row of steel wavers, the absence of tight stays, the flannel nightgown and blue wool bed-jacket, and the cold cream that glistened upon her mother's face and neck.

"Darling, you're very late. Who brought you home?"

"A girl called Mary Collier and her brother, and a—a friend of theirs, Captain Lane."

"Did you enjoy your evening?"

"Yes, awfully. It was great fun."

"I'm very glad. Now, drink some hot milk, and then off you go to bed. You'll lose all your freshness if you don't get enough sleep."

Mrs. Ingram lit the little spirit-lamp that stood in readiness on the bedside table, and heated the milk in the saucepan.

"Sit down a minute, just till your milk is ready, and tell me all about it."

Monica sat down on the arm of the easy-chair and gave her mother a detailed and lively account of everything in the evening that was of no importance whatever. When she could not remember, she invented, almost without knowing that she was doing so.

"Wasn't Claude Ashe very glad he'd been asked? Did he thank you for arranging it?"

"Oh yes, mother."

At the thought of Claude Ashe a dreadful sensation of mingled dismay, remorse, and impatience went through Monica. To think that she had felt excited, only a few hours earlier, because she was going to meet *him*!

"There—it's just not boiling. Pour it carefully into the cup, Monica, and then drink it while it's hot."

Monica obeyed. She wanted to be alone, in her own room, undisturbed except by the blissful chaos of her thoughts. She made none of her customary protests about the milk, and swallowed it nearly scalding.

"Good girl! Run along now, and you'd better have your breakfast in bed."

"Good-night, mother."

"Good-night, darling. I'm glad you enjoyed it so much."

Monica dutifully kissed her mother, and received and obeyed her injunctions to put out the light and shut the door quietly—and at last was free.

Parsons did not sit up for Monica unless her mistress was out as well, and as Monica had forgotten to ask her mother to unhook her dress she had to do it for herself, which took time and made her arms and shoulders ache. But she accomplished it at last, threw the dress over the back of a chair, and left all her other clothes in a heap on the floor. Then she had to wash, to take down her hair and brush it out, and finally to kneel down for her prayers.

An incoherent jumble of petitions came to her lips.

Please God, let it be all right . . . let him *really*. . . . Don't let anything spoil it. . . . I'll be so good, all my life, if only this can really and truly happen. . . .

At last she had turned out the light, and was in bed. She went over, again and again, everything that Christopher had said and looked and done. She felt sure that she had done wrong in allowing him to kiss her before he had actually proposed. Her mother would think it dreadful, and Monica was resolved that she should never, never know of it.

It was a long while before she felt in the least sleepy. A rapturous excitement possessed her and kept her tossing from side to side, re-living in imagination the evening that was, she decided, the most wonderful evening that her life could ever hold.

CHAPTER VI

MONICA slept late the next morning.
When she woke it was to a sense of throbbing excitement that at first bewildered her.

Then she remembered:

Christopher!

And she was to see him again in the afternoon.

Perhaps, thought Monica with awe, by this time to-morrow she would be engaged to be married.

But she felt no desire to play the old game of pretending to choose her wedding-dress and the colour scheme for the bridesmaids. She did not want to think about anything at all, excepting Christopher, and the feeling of his hand clasped over hers, and the way he had looked down into her eyes just before kissing her.

She was not at all certain that she wanted him to kiss her again. For one thing, it troubled her conscience very much indeed. She could almost hear her mother's voice, saying that no young man *ever* respected a girl who made herself cheap. No young man ever wanted such a girl to marry him. He merely despised her.

That didn't, and couldn't, apply to Christopher—but still, Monica was convinced that she had done wrong. She breathed a fervent petition that God would not punish her by letting Christopher stop caring about her.

There was a knock at the door and the housemaid entered with a can of hot water.

She drew back the pink curtains and pulled up the blind.

"Oh!" cried Monica involuntarily. "It isn't *raining*, is it?"

"Pouring, Miss Monica. It's been coming down hard ever since six o'clock."

It seemed too bad to be true.

How on earth could one hope to be taken to Hurlingham in pouring rain?

A terrible constriction in her throat warned Monica that she was very near to the ignominy of tears.

She lay down again, her face turned away from the window, and did not move until Mary had put down the breakfast tray and gone away again.

At eleven o'clock it was still raining.

At twelve, Mrs. Ingram said:

"Why don't you telephone to Frederica Marlow, and see if she and Cecily are doing anything this afternoon? If not, you might arrange something together."

"I thought we were going to Hurlingham," said Monica faintly.

"It's too wet, darling."

"I think it's clearing."

Mrs. Ingram, surprised, glanced first at Monica's face and then out of the drawing-room window. Rain still dripped from the black railings of the balcony, the pavements shone with wet, and the sky was leaden.

But it was true that it had stopped raining.

"Should you be very disappointed if we didn't go?" she enquired doubtfully.

"Well, I should, rather. I do like Hurlingham, and it's the last time we shall be able to go this year," Monica faltered, very anxious to say neither too much nor too little.

Her mother laughed indulgently.

"We'll see what it looks like after lunch. If the sun comes out, it might be possible—although I don't like you to get your feet wet."

The sun did come out.

Monica, in an ecstasy, thanked God.

"I really don't know what to say," Mrs. Ingram declared, just before one o'clock. "It certainly seems to be clearing up now, but it's *bound* to be wet underfoot."

"Is that Hurlingham?" Vernon Ingram enquired. "I think

81

I could come with you this afternoon. I should like to do that."

Monica's heart bounded. That, she knew, would settle it. If her father offered to escort them, and said that he would like to go to Hurlingham, then Hurlingham it would be.

It was.

Wandering demurely about the grounds with her parents, Monica exchanged polite greetings with their friends, and with one or two of her own.

She saw Mary Collier, conspicuous by reason of her curiously marked air of distinction and upright carriage, walking with a good-looking, tall man, of whom Vernon Ingram said:

"That's Lord Culmstock, whose father used to be a friend of mine many years ago. One of the most eligible young men in London."

"Is that the girl you met last night, Monica?" her mother asked.

"Yes. Miss Collier."

"I thought so. I heard there was someone," said Mrs. Ingram, with a mixture of satisfaction at having her information confirmed, and annoyance at the good fortune of somebody else's daughter.

Monica paid very little attention. She was absorbed in watching for Christopher Lane. Every time that she caught sight in the distance of an unusually tall man her heart beat faster, until she saw that it was not Christopher.

Presently they sat down to watch the game.

"He'll never find us here," Monica reflected despairingly.

They were joined by Lady Margaret Miller, and two gentlemen whom Monica instantly dismissed from her consciousness as being elderly and uninteresting, although one of them sat beside her and took pains to talk to her with the elaborate kindliness and entire lack of conviction characteristic of the conversation addressed to a *débutante* by her seniors.

Quite suddenly she saw Christopher. He was by himself, within four feet of her chair.

Monica felt herself changing colour. She bowed uncertainly, and he raised his hat and approached her.

Mrs. Ingram turned.

"Mother, this is Captain Lane," said Monica in a small voice. She remembered with relief that Lady Margaret Miller also knew him. That would, she knew, predispose her mother in his favour.

"Wake up, darling," said her mother's voice, laughing, but with an edge of sharpness to it.

Monica, realizing that she had momentarily lost herself, started violently.

"Captain Lane is asking if you would like to walk about a little. Joan and Peter are somewhere about, you might see if you can come across them."

Monica rose. She walked away beside Christopher Lane. Now that her almost terrifyingly intense desire to meet him again was fulfilled, she suddenly felt drained of all vitality, and incapable of speech.

They paced slowly along without speaking.

"Well," said Captain Lane at last—and at the first sound of his voice, it was as though the blood had begun to flow through her veins once more—"are you glad to see me again? I can't tell you how furious I was when I saw the rain this morning. I was afraid you mightn't come."

"I very nearly didn't."

"Would you have been disappointed?"

"Frightfully."

"Tell me why."

Monica looked up at him from under the brim of her large shady hat—white lace, trimmed with pink velvet cherries.

"You know."

"I don't think I do. Besides, I should like to hear you say it."

He was talking exactly like the people in books, and Monica felt as though she were herself a girl in a book—only no one, either in a book or outside it, had ever been so radiantly happy as she felt.

They talked and talked. Christopher told her things about himself—he had very little money, and he wanted to get on in his profession, and he thought that his Regiment would be going to India in the autumn—his people did not altogether understand him, and he saw very little of them—and he had never met anyone in the world who understood everything he said, as Monica did. Did she feel that too?

Monica felt that, and a great deal more besides. In a confused and agitated turmoil, she signified that she, too, had always been lonely. Her mother, even, did not really understand her. She had no brothers or sisters. No *really* intimate friends, even, because almost everybody, somehow, was rather disappointing when it came to the things that mattered most.

Presently, without knowing how it had happened, Monica found herself having tea with him at a little table, amongst a crowd of other little tables.

She was past wondering whether her parents would be displeased with her or not. She had temporarily forgotten their existence. She was recalled to earth by a greeting, spoken almost in her ear.

"Hullo, Monica!"

It was Alice Ashe, Claude's sister.

She was a tall, plain girl, several years older than her brother, good-natured, and not very intelligent.

She had appeared to take a fancy to Monica at their first meeting, and had suggested that they should exchange Christian names.

Monica introduced Captain Lane, because she did not know what else to do. Alice seemed to be by herself, and she sat happily down at their table. The conversation became unreal and manufactured.

At last Monica said unhappily:

"I expect I'd better find mother again. She'll think I'm lost."

"Let me take you back."

"Yes, come on," said Alice. "Claude is somewhere about, Monica. I'm sure he'd love to see you."

84

Monica was far from wishing to see Claude. She had a vague feeling of self-reproach and uneasiness in regard to Claude. He had certainly seemed vexed and upset after the expedition to Olympia, and she remembered that, since it was she who had procured the invitation for him, he might reasonably have expected to spend at least part of the evening with her. And she had been all the time with Christopher Lane.

Monica felt more and more like a girl in a book.

To her relief, they did not meet Claude. Lane, however, just as they came within sight of Monica's father and mother, saw some people whom he knew, and excused himself. As he lifted his hat, his glance at Monica was eloquent. They had already discovered that they were to meet at a dance—the last one of the season, for Monica—at the Ritz at the end of the week, and Christopher had made her promise to keep every third dance for him, and go down with him to supper.

In a dim and remote way—since nothing seemed quite real to her—Monica wondered whether Frederica and Cecily would be astonished, if they could know what was happening to her.

The moment she saw her mother's face, Monica realized that she was slightly in disgrace, although Mrs. Ingram said nothing at all except: "Well, darling, here you are," in a very bright voice.

She greeted Alice Ashe with warmth, and made many enquiries for Mrs. Ashe, whom she said she had not seen for years.

"Mummy never comes to London now. She's not very strong, I'm sorry to say."

"I'm sure you're a great help to her."

"I try to be, of course," said Alice, with a smile that showed all her teeth—very white ones, but also large and prominent.

It was that smile, Monica felt certain, that caused Mrs. Ingram to say emphatically on the way home that Alice Ashe seemed to be a particularly nice girl. It was probably the smile, also, that caused her father to reply, with very much tempered enthusiasm, that Alice seemed very nice indeed but that her looks—poor thing—were not her strong point.

He glanced at Monica as he spoke, as though involuntarily, and although she was careful to look as unconscious as possible, the tribute that she divined gratified her vanity. Prettiness, Monica had always heard, was not invariably the thing that attracted men most easily, but of course, it was important, and it was nice to know that one had up-curled eyelashes, and a good complexion, and wasn't too short, or too tall, or too fat, or too thin.

When they reached home, Monica, still apprehensive, attempted to go straight upstairs.

"Just wait a minute, dear. I want to speak to you."

It was a formula that, coming from either of her parents, never failed to cause Monica's heart to sink.

She meekly followed Mrs. Ingram into the library.

"Were you with that Captain Lane all the afternoon?"

"Well—only part of it. Part of the time I was with you and father."

"Naturally, I know you were. But I mean, of course, when you went off like that."

"Well, I was—we just—Alice Ashe was there, quite a lot."

"That has nothing to do with what I'm asking you. I'm not at all angry with you, Monica, but I want you to give me a straightforward answer to my question at once. Were you, or were you not, with Captain Lane all that time?"

Monica debated the advantages and disadvantages of telling a lie, and decided immediately that she was not likely to be able to tell a convincing one. So she looked down at her white kid gloves, twisted them into a ball between her hands, and said, with a mixture of sullenness and defiance:

"Yes. I was."

"Very well, darling. Quite right to tell mother the truth, and I'm not in the least vexed with you. But I want to talk to you a little, about this Captain Lane."

86

Monica's heart, already in her buckled shoes, seemed, at this, ready to sink through the floor.

"Sit down, my pet."

"I'd rather stand."

"Mother said Sit down, Monica."

Monica sat.

"Now listen to me, my darling. I've been hearing something about this Captain Lane, and he hasn't got a very good reputation. There may be no real harm in him—I dare say there isn't—but he's not a friend I very much care about for you. I suppose you met him at Lady Margaret Miller's house last night?"

"Yes."

" 'Yes, mother.' Well, if you've only met him once before, there's no special need to go out of your way to have anything more to do with him. Be polite, of course, but don't go off by yourself with him as you did this afternoon, and don't dance with him."

"But mother———" Monica felt that her face was scarlet, and her voice full of consternation.

"Well?" Mrs. Ingram sounded slightly amused, but also slightly impatient.

"Why isn't he—why mayn't I—— Has he done anything wrong?"

"Not that I know of," Mrs. Ingram replied serenely. "But I don't very much care for what I hear about him, and, in any case, he's not anybody at all. 'Lane' means absolutely nothing. He might be anybody or nobody—and he certainly isn't anybody. Tell me, what did he talk to you about this afternoon?"

"Nothing, mother."

"My dear child, don't answer me like that. It's not only childish, it's almost impertinent. How could you and Captain Lane have spent over two hours talking about nothing?"

How indeed?

Monica, confused, guilty, helpless, and terribly afraid of bursting into tears if she spoke at all, remained silent.

Her mother made a short, vexed sound that was not quite a laugh.

"I'm afraid I've made a great mistake in letting you have all this modern freedom. If I'd been as strict with you as Lady Marlowe is with Frederica and Cecily, this would never have happened. Now, no more nonsense, Monica. I'm only too glad that you should enjoy yourself and make friends, but they must be friends that mother likes. The Ashes, now . . . I'm afraid poor Claude Ashe didn't have a very amusing evening at the Exhibition."

Monica understood that Lady Margaret, probably quite good-naturedly, had been talking.

"It doesn't do a young man any harm to see that a girl isn't running after him, and can have other friends if she wants them—but at the same time, it's very bad form to drop an old friend for the sake of a new one—especially in the case of a young girl. I don't say there's any great harm done, where Claude Ashe is concerned—he wouldn't ever be any *real* use, anyway. Now that's all, Monica. I'm not angry with you—it's natural you should make mistakes at your age, and who's to tell you about them, if not your own mother?"

There was, as Monica and Mrs. Ingram both knew well, no answer to this enquiry.

"Run along and change your shoes," Mrs. Ingram brightly admonished her daughter. "And your stockings too, if they're damp. In fact, you'd better dress for dinner at once, it's not really much too early."

Monica swallowed a hard lump in her throat, went to the door, opened it, and then turned round.

"Do you want me to—to *cut* Captain Lane?" she asked, in a loud, unnatural voice.

"Monica! Haven't you listened to a *word* I've been saying? Of course you're to be polite. Only if he asks you to dance or anything, just say you're engaged. Never mind whether you are or not. He'll understand."

"Mayn't I even know why?"

"Why? Because he's a young man whom it won't do you

88

any good to be seen about with. I've asked one or two people about him, and they all agree that he's much too apt to make young girls conspicuous by attentions that mean nothing at all. In any case, he hasn't any money, and couldn't possibly think of marrying. He's no use whatever."

Monica, after looking dumbly at her mother for another moment, went out of the room.

Upstairs in her bedroom, she locked her door—although not allowed to do so—and broke into a violent fit of crying, prolonging it until long after her tears had ceased to be a relief, and had almost become an effort.

Alternately, she rebelled and despaired.

She made up speeches—defiant, courageous, and yet reasonable speeches—that would force her parents to see once and for all that she had no intention of giving up Christopher whatever *anybody* might say—and evolved a confused, fantastic story, of which she was herself the heroine, about an elopement and secret marriage.

Every now and then, as a sob shook her, she realized afresh that in less than a week she was to be taken away from London, and that before she came back again, Christopher would have sailed for India.

(This final contingency sounded so romantic that Monica adopted it as a probability, although Christopher had said that most likely the Regiment would not sail before November.)

There was still the ball at the Ritz. If only one had been going there with a party! But Mrs. Ingram was taking Monica on, after a reception, and would herself chaperon her daughter.

"I must write to him," thought Monica.

The decision comforted her a little. Moreover it was now quite impossible to cry any more, and she must dress for dinner.

With some reluctance she got up from the bed, saw with a certain satisfaction that her tears had made an enormous wet patch on the pillow, and called "Come in!" to Mary with the hot water.

Careful sponging removed most of the traces of weeping from Monica's face. She did her hair again, changed into the high-necked white frock that she wore on the evenings when the Ingrams were alone, and went downstairs.

Both her parents were already in the drawing-room. In less than five minutes Monica had realized with surprise that her mother must have been talking to her father, that both of them were feeling rather sorry for her, and were endeavouring, by extra kindliness of manner, to console her for what—she supposed bitterly—they doubtless viewed as her childish disappointment and mortification.

They talked of things that were supposed to interest her during dinner, and afterwards her father did not suggest a Bridge-lesson, but said that he would go to the Club for a rubber, and patted her on the shoulder as he kissed her good-night.

"I should read a book on the sofa, darling, if I were you," said Mrs. Ingram. "And go up to bed early. All these late nights have made you look a little bit washed out."

Monica obeyed, feeling grateful in a dim, exhausted way.

At half-past nine her mother sent her upstairs.

"I'll come and tuck you up in a quarter of an hour," said Mrs. Ingram—which meant that in a quarter of an hour Monica's light would be extinguished, with a tacit prohibition against turning it on again that night.

She undressed, and brushed and plaited her hair as quickly as possible, then knelt to say her prayers.

A rush of confused petitions was succeeded by a kind of tangled explanation, addressed rather to Monica's conscience than to her God, concerning the letter that she intended to write, in order that Christopher might know at once what had happened. This might, in a way, seem wrong, unmaidenly, disobedient, and even deceitful—but God must understand, and help her, and, above all, must not allow her mother to guess anything at all. Monica then added her usual nightly formula and got into bed.

"Good-night, my pet," said her mother.

"Good-night, mother," Monica made her voice sound as sleepy as possible.

But Mrs. Ingram lingered.

"Don't let your little self worry over what I said to you this afternoon. It's quite natural you should make mistakes at your age, and there's no harm done. I dare say we shall meet some quite worthwhile people this summer and autumn, and you've got one or two friends already, haven't you?"

"Yes, mother."

"We must get Claude Ashe and Alice to come and do a theatre with us one night when we get back again after Scotland. I thought she seemed such a nice girl."

"Yes. Thank you very much, mother."

"Good-night then, darling. Go to sleep. God bless you."

Mrs. Ingram kissed Monica, put out the light, and went away, softly closing the door behind her.

Monica, gritting her teeth, lay in the darkness.

Experience had taught her that it wasn't worth while to turn the light on again. Mrs. Ingram had a tendency to hear mysterious noises in the evening, and to make frequent expeditions both upstairs and down. A bar of light showing beneath Monica's bedroom door would attract her attention without fail, and probably bring her into the room again for an explanation.

It was not possible to cry any more—Monica had exhausted her capacity for tears earlier in the evening. She thought about Christopher Lane, recalling everything that she could of all he had said to her that afternoon, and gradually falling into a state between sleeping and waking, in which she evolved a series of fantastic situations, ending in an elopement and marriage, and her return home to break the news to her parents, wearing a wedding-ring and with Christopher beside her.

The next morning she wrote her letter.

It proved more difficult than she had expected. To begin with, she did not know what to call him. "Captain Lane" seemed unnatural to a degree, but she had never yet said

"Christopher" except to herself. Finally she decided to have no formal beginning at all.

"I am in great trouble," she wrote. "I may not have a chance of dancing with you or even *speaking* to you, at the Ritz on Friday, and I do so want to explain what has happened. Nothing can make any real difference to our friendship, but things are being made very difficulty for me at home. I only wish I could see you, and tell you about it all, but I suppose there's no chance of that, unless you're going to any of the places I'm going to?"

Here Monica gave a detailed list of such engagements as she knew had been made for the coming week, omitting those to be undertaken with her mother only.

None of them, seen from her present point of view, appeared very hopeful, excepting an appointment with the dentist at eleven o'clock on Wednesday to which she would have to be escorted by one of the maids, since Mrs. Ingram had an engagement at the same hour, in the opposite direction, with her dressmaker. It would surely be possible for Christopher to be walking up Brook Street at five minutes to eleven on Wednesday morning. . . .

Monica did not make this suggestion, but she prayed fervently that Christopher might make it.

On the way to church she posted her letter, sandwiched discreetly between a letter addressed to her old governess and a picture-postcard to a small cousin who collected them. Actually, her mother had long ago given up any systematic supervision of Monica's correspondence, but occasionally, unexpectedly, she did scrutinize an envelope, or desire to be shown its contents.

Monica decided that she could not possibly get any reply from Christopher until Tuesday morning at the earliest. Nevertheless, she began to glance anxiously at the letters on the hall-table mid-day on Monday. She did not even know his handwriting by sight, but the postmark would be Woolwich.

No letter came on Monday, and she woke very early on

Tuesday morning, her heart already beating quickly in anticipation.

Letters were never brought up to her room, but laid in her place at the breakfast table.

She went down early.

Nothing—excepting a note from Frederica Marlowe concerning a tea-party, and an offer of a complimentary sitting from a fashionable photographer.

Monica felt herself turning very hot and then very cold. She sat silently through breakfast, sick and numbed with disappointment. She felt, now, that no letter from Christopher would ever come at all.

Nor did it.

The realization that he had not answered her appeal caused her far greater and more real suffering than the unhappiness she had felt at being told that she was to have nothing more to do with him. *That* unhappiness, she knew now, had been alleviated by the consciousness of persecution, and the sense of being the heroine of a romance.

Everything that she had ever been told of the contempt in which men held a girl who "made herself cheap" came back to her, hurting and humiliating her unbearably.

On Wednesday morning it rained, and Mary the house-maid, in her neat black, escorted Miss Monica in a four-wheeled cab to Brook Street.

Monica glanced forlornly up and down the street, but there was no one to be seen except a policeman, and a couple of ladies under an umbrella, far down the wet pavement.

She followed the man-servant into the waiting-room.

A tall man, sitting near the window, rose as she came in. It was Christopher Lane.

CHAPTER VII

Monica's romance lasted exactly a week, from the moment that Christopher, whilst the maid was still paying the cab, suggested that she should be sent to do an errand.

"But what?" gasped Monica.

"To buy a book—anything. Whatever sounds natural."

It did not seem to Monica that anything could sound natural, but she remembered that she did want a new sponge-bag and a fine comb, and in an oddly wavering voice she suggested that Mary should "save time" by going in search of these articles.

Mary looked rather surprised, but the rain had stopped, and possibly, although this did not occur to Monica, she was not averse from a walk in the streets by herself.

She obediently went out again.

"You poor little darling," said Christopher's deep voice, "what have they been doing to you?"

Bliss invaded Monica's whole being. She surrendered in that instant, without knowing that she had done so, her shallow, youthful judgment—that only owed such stability as it possessed to the careful efforts of her parents—in exchange for all the ecstasies of first love, and all the rapturous excitement of conducting an illicit emotional adventure unknown to the authorities that had hitherto governed every moment of her life.

The quarter of an hour in the waiting-room passed like a flash; but before it was over Monica had promised to try and come to the National Gallery on the following morning and meet Christopher there. It was, he said, extremely important that he should speak to her. He had something to say to her.

"Aren't you ever allowed to go anywhere alone?" he demanded.

"No. But I think I could bring another girl who—who wouldn't be in the way: Cecily Marlowe."

He shook his head.

"Better not. She'd know who I was, quite well, and might easily say something that would get you into trouble afterwards. That," said Christopher, "is the one thing that I couldn't bear. No, bring your maid again. I could square her if necessary."

In spite of herself, Monica was shocked, and felt the suggestion to be a vulgar one. To bribe a servant to hold her tongue!

Christopher was quick to see his mistake.

"Don't look so scared, my pretty one, it'll be all right. You can tell her to go and look at the pictures in the other galleries, or something. I'll meet you in No. 1, as near twelve o'clock as you can manage it."

He pressed her hand, and his touch, disturbing Monica in a way new and enthralling, drove everything else from her mind.

She met him in the National Gallery, exactly as he had suggested. Mary, by what Monica regarded as a piece of phenomenal good fortune, had a bad foot, and it was quite natural to tell her, as considerately as possible, to sit down on one of the seats and rest her foot, whilst Monica went and looked at the pictures.

She had wondered what it was that Christopher had to tell her—but when they were together, she forgot about it, and no special communication was ever made.

She and Christopher talked about themselves, and he told her that she was the most wonderful girl he had ever met, and that he needed an influence like hers in his life. He did not ask her to marry him, and Monica did not really know whether they were engaged or not. Somehow it hardly seemed to matter. In any case she knew now that her parents would not allow her to marry Christopher. Her mother had as good as said so. They wanted her to marry, of course, but they didn't want her to choose for herself, she thought scornfully.

She was living in a dream, unable to see beyond the ball at the Ritz that was, so far as they could tell, to be their last opportunity of meeting before Monica went away. The ball was to be on Friday, and she was travelling down to Sussex with her father and mother on Saturday afternoon.

She had told Christopher—after resolving not to—exactly what her mother had said to her about him, and the prohibition as to dancing with him.

"People are very unjust, sometimes," he said quietly. "I know that one or two mothers have taken up the attitude that I'm not a fit person to trust their daughters with, even for a dance."

"But why?"

"I'll tell you about it some day, Monica, if you'll let me. I'd like to tell you, because I know you'll understand. But about Friday night. . . ."

He told her that there was a place for sitting-out on the roof at the Ritz, a garden covered in by an awning. Would she meet him up there for the tenth dance, keeping that and two subsequent ones free? Her mother would almost certainly be in the supper-room then.

Monica promised.

It seemed to her that this was to be the culminating point of her existence. Her imagination refused to envisage anything at all beyond it.

On the day before the ball Frederica and Cecily came round to Eaton Square to say good-bye. They were going with their mother to Oxfordshire.

"Monica," said Frederica, "what about Claude Ashe?"

Monica started before she could control herself. She had forgotten all about Claude Ashe.

"Nothing," she said, in confusion.

"Alice Ashe says that you wouldn't have anything to do with him, the night you went to the White City. She says he's frightfully hurt about it."

"It shows how much he likes you," Cecily put in. "Perhaps he's really in earnest, Monica."

"He couldn't be," Frederica interposed quickly. "He can't afford to marry—at least, not for years and years."

"Oh, Monica," Cecily entreated, "do tell us if he's proposed and you've refused him."

Monica was very much tempted to reply that she had. She was practically certain that neither of the Marlowes had ever received a proposal, and she knew that if she said that she had, it would fill Frederica's heart with envy and Cecily's with wistful admiration.

But the risk of discovery was much too great, if she perpetrated so obvious a fraud. She contented herself with a reply implying that only her own tact and determination had averted an offer of marriage from Claude.

"I don't think it's fair," said Monica grandly, "to let a man actually come to the point, if one doesn't mean to accept him in the end."

"Of course not," said Frederica. But she said it without conviction, and Monica knew very well that, to Cecily and her sister, she had now become one of that mysterious and fortunate band of "girls who were attractive to men."

What would they have said if they could have known about Christopher? At the mere thought of him, a soft glow seemed to diffuse itself all over Monica.

She could not resist talking round the subject of the ball on Friday, to which the Marlowes were not going; but they were not interested. They were scarcely interested in anything excepting themselves, their mother's moods, and the difficulty of ever getting married.

When they got up to leave, Frederica said that it would be nice to have Monica to stay, and the girls exchanged their customary meaningless embrace. Frederica's kiss was as limp and flaccid as her hand-shake, given with half-open mouth, like a child's. Cecily, rigid with her distaste for physical contact, never kissed one at all, but touched one's face with her own, forcing herself to do it because it was

97

expected of her. Monica had often wanted to tell her not to—that it didn't matter—but, in point of fact, she thought it did matter, because both her own mother and Cecily's would have required an explanation, if either had perceived any omission in the conventional signs of affection.

"Good-bye, Fricky. I'm awfully looking forward to coming to stay. Shall I bring tennis things?"

"Oh yes. I should. Have you got a racquet?"

"I think I have."

"Well, if not, we can lend you one. Good-bye, Monica."

"Good-bye," repeated Cecily. "I hope your house-parties will be fun."

"I'll write and tell you about them."

They were gone, and Monica viewed their departure, as she did everything else, as one more landmark left behind on the way to Friday night and the roof-garden.

It came at last.

"I shan't stay late to-night," said Mrs. Ingram, adjusting her black velvet shoulder-straps, and then smartly tucking a lace handkerchief out of sight down the front of her *décolletage*.

"How late, mother?"

"Well—certainly not after one. So don't book too many dances, my child."

How little she knows, thought Monica sentimentally, treasuring the anticipation of the tenth dance and the two following ones, already promised to Christopher.

In the ball-room, she found that she did not know many people, and that her programme did not fill up.

Mrs. Ingram began to look anxious.

"Stand forward, Monica. No one can see you there. Get right in front of me, at once."

Monica, feeling extremely self-conscious, stood forward, and pretended absorption in the buttoning of her long white kid gloves.

"Don't bend your head down like that!" came, in a sharp whisper, from her mother behind her. "Be ready to catch the eye of anyone you know."

Suddenly Monica saw Claude Ashe. He bowed, hesitated, and then came up and asked her for a dance.

"May I have number seven with you?"

"Yes, certainly," said Monica, handing him her programme. He put down his initials.

She still had several dances left unclaimed.

Mrs. Ingram, talking to a dowager, presented Monica, and explained that her daughter was "only just out" and knew very few men in the room.

"Let me introduce one or two of my party," said the old lady good-naturedly.

She captured two partners for Monica, and then Mr. Pelham appeared and asked her for a two-step. She thought him very dull, but accepted eagerly, anxious to escape the humiliation and tedium of having to stand out a dance.

"Show me your programme," said her mother. "How's it getting on? Oh, that's better."

Monica had left everything blank after the ninth number.

"You'd better not book any more after supper."

Monica's partner claimed her, and saved her from the necessity of replying.

"And how do you enjoy being grown-up?" said Mr. Pelham, exactly as he had said every time that he had had any conversation with Monica ever since their first meeting.

"I like it very much."

"I suppose you've been having a very gay time?"

"Yes, I've had great fun. Of course, the season is really over now, isn't it?"

Monica was speaking quite mechanically. She had caught sight of Christopher, and a delicious turmoil had invaded her. He was dancing with a girl in white—not pretty, Monica decided with relief—and in another moment or two it seemed certain that the two couples would pass one another. Mr. Pelham, gripping Monica rather too firmly, was steering her round and round in a determined, uninspiring dance.

They were close to Christopher and his partner.

". . . any amount of tennis," said the voice of Mr. Pelham, seeming very far away.

"Yes—oh, yes."

Monica's eyes and Christopher's had met, had held one another's gaze for a breath-taking instant.

"Then, if I accept Lady Marlowe's very kind invitation for the last week-end in the month, I hope to have the pleasure of meeting you."

"That will be delightful," Monica replied, with only a dim understanding of what it was that would be delightful.

The dance came to an end.

"Shall we find somewhere to sit down?"

They wandered, rather vaguely, in the wake of other couples. Some men always found one a comfortable seat in an interesting sitting-out place at once—and others never did. Monica knew already that Mr. Pelham belonged to the latter category. Sure enough, every alcove, every sofa and arm-chair, was already occupied, and they were obliged to content themselves with two upright gilt chairs in a rather draughty corridor. Then Mr. Pelham, painstakingly, produced remarks about the band, the state of the floor, the number of people present, and the superiority of the country to the town in the months of July and August.

Monica offered perfunctory assents.

"The other day," remarked Mr. Pelham, "I heard of a fellow who was sitting out a dance with a girl. They'd talked about all the usual things and didn't seem to have anything more to say, and whatever he asked her she only seemed to answer Yes or No—so what do you think he suddenly said?"

"What?"

"He suddenly asked her: '*Do you like string?*' Without any preliminary, you know," said Mr. Pelham, with a joyless appreciation of his own anecdote. "Just '*Do you like string?*' he suddenly said."

Monica, startled into attention, laughed uncertainly.

"It was so absolutely pointless, you see," Mr. Pelham explained. "They'd talked about all the usual things and didn't seem to have anything more to say, and so he just asked her, quite suddenly, 'Do you like string?' "

"What did she answer?"

"I don't know."

There was a silence, until Monica, afraid lest he might guess that she was bewildered rather than amused, repeated: "Do you like string?" and then laughed again, and said: "Yes, that's rather nice."

"I don't know what made me think of it just now," her partner said. "But it struck me as being rather good. So absolutely silly, you know. *Do you like string?*"

He paid a further tribute of reflective laughter to his *mot*, in which Monica politely joined.

Then the interval was over, and Claude Ashe, standing in front of Monica, was saying formally:

"This is our dance, Miss Ingram, I believe."

"Well, thank you very much," said Mr. Pelham, and bowed as he turned away.

In the relief of finding herself with someone of her own age again, Monica sprang up, glad to let Claude take her back into the ball-room and begin dancing with her. She even spoke to him quite naturally, and without the self-consciousness usually inseparable from conversation with a man.

"I hardly know anybody here to-night and it's the last dance I'm going to before we leave London; isn't it a shame?'

"Yes, rather. I don't know many people either."

He paused, and Monica with a rush of returning self-consciousness thought with dismay that he might have interpreted her words into a hint that she had other dances to spare. How *dreadful*, if he should suppose that she wanted him to ask her for another dance!

Claude's next words, however, showed him to have been thinking of something else.

"I really came to-night because I knew I should see you, and I—I wanted to ask you something."

A pulse leapt in Monica's throat.

Could he possibly be going to ask her to marry him?

To refuse even an entirely ineligible proposal in one's first season would be a triumph. Mrs. Ingram would feel that her child was being a success, and would see to it that nobody who mattered remained unaware that Monica "had had a chance."

"Did you?" she asked faintly.

"Yes. Have I—have I done anything to offend you?"

"Of course not."

Monica's elation left her as suddenly as it had come. She felt certain now that Claude Ashe, far from asking her to marry him, was going to demand an explanation of her ungracious avoidance of him—and she had no explanation to offer. A still more childish apprehension disturbed her. If Claude Ashe were seriously offended he might tell his sister Alice—perhaps he had done so already—and it would all come round to Monica's mother, and she would certainly be vexed, and scold Monica. Scoldings from her mother still ranked as calamities in Monica's estimation.

Claude Ashe, rather awkwardly, was elaborating his enquiry.

"I hope you don't think me rude for speaking like this, but you see I really have felt most awfully worried about it. You see, I didn't know what it was I'd done, exactly, but I felt sure that there must be *something*."

"Oh no," murmured Monica unconvincingly.

They bumped into another couple.

"I beg your pardon," apologized Claude.

"You see, I don't seem to have seen anything of you the last time or two we've met, and I was afraid you might be annoyed about something or other."

"But why should I be?"

"Oh, I don't know."

Deadlock appeared to have been reached. They continued to dance in mutual dissatisfaction.

Monica, passing her mother, received a smile and almost imperceptible nod of approval. Mrs. Ingram was talking to

102

an elderly man with a white moustache, and evidently point-ing out her daughter to him. His slight smile and appraising glance followed her for a moment. Monica could almost hear his courteous comment: "Charming, indeed! Quite charming!"

It did not very much elate her. Old gentlemen always said that kind of thing, and, anyway, old gentlemen were not interesting.

Nothing was of the least importance, excepting the fact that the moment when she was to be with Christopher was coming, however slowly, nearer and nearer.

Even Claude's anxious attempts at establishing an under-standing between them seemed to matter very little.

"You're sure you aren't annoyed with me about any-thing?" he repeated.

"Of course not."

"I was awfully disappointed that night we went to the White City. I never saw anything of you at all."

"I—I couldn't help it. I didn't know you'd mind," faltered Monica. Out of the tail of her eye she looked for her mother. If she went down to supper now it would be much too early, and she might be back in the ball-room when Christopher came to fetch Monica. But no, it was all right—Mrs. Ingram had not moved.

And Claude's dance had come to an end.

They secured arm-chairs under a large palm that stood behind a high screen.

"May I get you an ice or something?"

"Yes please. I'd like something to drink. Lemonade or something, please."

She watched him go with thankfulness. She did not want the lemonade. She wanted to be alone, so that she could think about Christopher and abandon herself blissfully to the rap-turous anticipations that possessed her.

Claude Ashe came back only too soon.

"I don't think this dance is going awfully well, do you? I mean, people are leaving already. Of course I'm enjoying it tremendously myself," he added hastily.

Monica inwardly fell into an agony.

If people were leaving, then her mother would be certain to want to go very early indeed—even earlier than she had said. And Monica could not even plead that her programme was full, for she had no dances booked between the one that had just ended and numbers ten, eleven, twelve, and thirteen —left blank on the programme, but promised to Christopher.

She was almost in despair when Claude took her back to the ball-room again.

"Shall we find Mrs. Ingram?"

"I'm going to meet my partner here," lied Monica, taking her stand in the doorway, and hoping to remain there unobserved until her mother should have gone safely to the supper-room. She looked round for Christopher Lane but he was nowhere to be seen.

"I say, I hope we shall meet again before you go away," said Claude Ashe, lingering.

"Yes, I do hope so."

"Shall you be in the Park to-morrow by any chance?"

"We might be, after tea. Or perhaps in the morning. That's no good for you though, is it?"

"I'm afraid not. But I shall try my luck round about six o'clock if I possibly can. There's my partner looking for me, I'm afraid."

Monica forgot him the moment after he had moved away.

If only she could see Christopher, perhaps they could slip away now, instead of waiting for Number Ten. The group of people round the door was thinning rapidly and the couples dancing were not very numerous. Claude Ashe had been right: people were leaving early.

Monica pressed herself closer against the wall. Usually she felt terribly self-conscious if she had to stand out a dance, but now she was aware of nothing at all except an anxious desire to escape her mother's observation and to find Christopher. She began to pray frenziedly and incoherently:

"O God, let him come quickly. O do let him come now before mother sees me—please, *please*, God. I'll be so good if only you'll grant me just this one thing . . . please, God. Send Christopher here now, this minute. . . ."

God had answered her prayer!

Christopher was at her elbow.

"Aren't you dancing this one? May I have it?"

"Yes, oh yes," she gasped. And, true to the tradition that she must always, always appear to be in request, Monica added breathlessly:

"I expect my partner made a muddle—or I did—he hasn't turned up——"

She followed Christopher Lane out of the ball-room—followed him blindly and with a wildly beating heart, up and up, until they emerged into a dimly-lit coolness, a deserted square of roof-garden, tented in with an awning and furnished with wicker chairs and cushions. Christopher, seeming to tower in the low-roofed enclosure, cast a swift glance round.

"We've got it to ourselves, thank Heaven!"

He turned to face Monica.

She did not know exactly what it was that she expected, but Christopher Lane gave her no time to wonder. He caught her in his arms and kissed her mouth and eyes passionately.

Completely carried away, Monica, her arms round his neck, her body pressed against his, returned his kisses. When at last his mouth released hers, Christopher almost lifted her to a chair, and sank down beside her, one hand clasping both of hers.

"Monica—darling—I love you."

"I love you," she whispered.

No one came to disturb them. Even the sound of the music far below was almost inaudible.

Monica let Christopher kiss her again and again. Intoxicated, she felt that for the first time she understood and was experiencing, the real meaning of life.

Time no longer existed.

It was with a violent start she was recalled to reality, when the roof-garden was invaded by half a dozen noisy intruders.

Monica, half lying in her lover's arms, sprang erect, and put both hands to her wildly disordered hair.

"Oh, I must go down. I don't know what time it is—how long we've been here——"

"It's all right, sweetheart, I'm sure it is."

He did not, however, attempt to detain her, and they went down the stairs.

Monica would have gone straight back to the ball-room, but Christopher laid a hand on her arm.

"I think you'd better slip into the ladies' dressing-room first," he said very low, and smiling at her. "Your hair just wants a touch."

Blushing hotly, Monica obeyed.

The cloak-room was empty, except for a maid who looked rather strangely at Monica.

She dared not linger, but put her hair in order as quickly as possible, and powdered her burning face. Her eyes shone back at her from the glass with an extraordinary effect of size and brilliancy.

Feeling certain that Christopher had waited for her in the corridor outside, Monica turned swiftly, and almost collided with her mother in the doorway

Unaware of the instant alteration in her own expression, Monica only realized that her mother was deeply disturbed.

"Monica! I've been looking for you everywhere. Where have you been?"

"I—I—Is it late?"

"Yes. Put on your cloak directly."

Involuntarily Monica's eyes went to the corridor beyond. Mrs. Ingram had swept past her into the cloak-room.

Christopher Lane was nowhere to be seen.

Monica and her mother received their wraps in silence, and in silence went to the entrance. Everywhere, lights were being extinguished. The brougham stood, almost alone, at the kerb.

Then the ball was over?

Monica dared not speak. She had never in her life been so

frightened, but underlying her fright and quite definite sense of guilt was the rapturous memory of what had happened. She could not feel that anything else would really matter in the end.

Her mother did not speak at all. She was very pale, and her lips were closely compressed. In the darkness of the narrow brougham she drew her fur-and-satin wrap closely round her shoulders and leant back in the corner, avoiding any contact with Monica.

Once, as the car took them swiftly down the empty breadth of Piccadilly, Monica attempted to speak.

"I'm very sorry——"

Mrs. Ingram winced, and put up her white-gloved hand in a quick movement.

"No, I don't want to hear anything at all until we get home."

Then they were to have it out at once—not wait until the morning? That, at least, was a relief.

Eaton Square was reached only too quickly.

As they passed through the hall, Monica saw that it was past three o'clock.

Mrs. Ingram went straight into the library, switched on one green-shaded reading-lamp, and shut the door behind Monica. Then she turned and faced her daughter.

Monica was prepared to hear that she had behaved disgracefully in disappearing from the ball-room, and in keeping her mother waiting interminably, and she had a graver fear that her mother knew, or meant to find out, with whom she had spent the evening. Beneath all her fear and shame exultation still possessed her, and she felt like the heroine of a novel. Moreover, she had made up her mind, swiftly and on impulse, to tell the truth. It would have to come out in the end, and her parents had better understand at once that she and Christopher were in earnest. They hadn't had time to discuss anything at all, reflected Monica in blissful astonishment, but they loved one another, and what else mattered?

She clenched her hands beneath her cloak, bracing herself to meet her mother's severity.

But Mrs. Ingram, after one long, unwavering look, astonished and terrified Monica by suddenly dropping into a chair, covering her face with her hands, and breaking into hard, irrepressible sobs.

CHAPTER VIII

It was not at once—it was not, indeed, for years—that Monica fully realized the disastrous results of her love-affair with Christopher Lane. Yet, even on her return home after the ball, she learnt something of the extent to which she had jeopardized her own chances of happiness and success in life.

Imogen Ingram, with tears pouring down her face, terrified her daughter the more because she was heartbroken rather than angry.

"How could you do it, Monica—how *could* you, darling? A man who isn't even a gentleman!"

"He is—he *is*!" Monica protested passionately, for she thought the accusation a most terrible one. To say that man wasn't a gentleman was to put him outside one's life altogether and for always.

"You know nothing about him—except that I told you to have nothing more to do with him. And now you see how right I was. As if a gentleman would ever have behaved like that to a young girl!"

For Mrs. Ingram had known, without questioning Monica at all, that Captain Lane had been her companion. Someone had seen them leaving the ball-room and had innocently said so when Mrs. Ingram began to enquire anxiously where Monica could be. No one, it appeared, had known about the sitting-out place on the roof.

"I went round everywhere, myself, as quietly as I could without letting anyone know what I was doing—but, naturally, I couldn't go over the whole of that huge building—and I hadn't any idea there *was* such a place as a roof-garden. Was anyone else up there?"

"Not at first. Right at the end, one or two people came up. No one I know," said Monica hastily. "Oh mother, I hadn't the least idea it was so late."

"Late! Everything was over. I had to pretend that you'd gone home with friends, and skulk about near the dressing-rooms, waiting for you—but it's no use hoping that people won't come to hear about it. That kind of thing always gets out, sooner or later."

"How?" faltered Monica.

"Do you suppose that a man like that is going to keep it to himself?" her mother enquired bitterly. "When a girl makes herself cheap, a young man loses his respect for her—naturally—and is quite ready to laugh about her with his friends afterwards."

"He's not like that."

"How do you know?" said her mother sharply. "You know nothing whatever about him, except that he has a very bad reputation and flirts with any girl who's weak and silly enough to give him the chance—and that he's behaved with you as a cad always does behave. Monica"—her mother drew a long breath—"it makes me perfectly sick to have to ask you such a thing, but I must do it. Did he take any liberties with you?"

Monica turned scarlet, and Mrs. Ingram, watching her narrowly, groaned.

"Did you allow him to kiss you?"

Monica burst into tears.

"What do you suppose father will say? Poor father, who's always been so proud of you!"

"Oh, don't, don't tell him."

"Of course I must tell him. How could I keep a thing like that from him? Besides, he'll have to see the young man, and let him understand that we know what's happened."

"But mother——"

"What?"

"Can't I—wouldn't you—— Shan't I—be engaged to him?"

"Has he asked you to?"

Monica was unable to remember that he had. She stared at her mother in a miserable consternation.

"But we're in love with one another," she said timidly, at last.

"My poor child, you don't know what you're talking about. A young man who's honourably in love with a girl asks her to marry him. He doesn't behave as he might behave with a—a vulgar little shop-girl. Oh Monica, my poor darling, I do pray God that you haven't destroyed your whole chances by this—this terrible business. If only we can keep people from finding out!"

Mrs. Ingram hid her face in her hands.

When at last she looked up and dried her eyes, there was an air of sheer exhaustion about her that terrified Monica still further.

"You must go to bed, and so must I. Don't come downstairs to-morrow morning. You can ring for breakfast when you wake up, and I'll come and see you later, after I've had a talk with father."

"What will he do?"

"I don't know. Whatever it is will be wise and right. Gentlemen know much more about these things than we do. And I shall try and persuade him not to see Captain Lane until he's got over the first shock of it all."

Mrs. Ingram, looking utterly worn out, preceded Monica upstairs. At the door of her own bedroom she paused and drew the girl towards her.

"My poor little thing, you know I'll do everything I can in the world to help you. I ought to have looked after you better."

"No, no," sobbed Monica, completely overwhelmed by a generosity that she had not expected and felt that she did not deserve. "Oh, please forgive me."

"Yes, I do forgive you, my poor darling. Good-night. God bless you. Try and sleep."

Opening the door very softly, Mrs. Ingram went into her room, and Monica, more tired out than ever in her life before, and now crying quite uncontrollably, dragged herself up-stairs, holding by the banisters all the way.

She slept far sooner than she had expected. Her last waking thought was that at least the worst was over now that discovery had come. She knew that sooner or later she would have to confront her father, but it seemed to her inconceivable that he should address her directly on so emotional a topic. They had always kept on the surface of things. He preferred it so, she felt certain.

Actually, when she woke, soon after eleven o'clock, Monica felt hopeful, although her eyelids were stiff from crying, and her head ached. Christopher had said he loved her. His kisses had been wonderful. Perhaps it was all going to come right, as things always did in books.

"By this time to-morrow," thought Monica, "I may be engaged."

Her first shock came when Parsons entered the room, and asked if she might do Miss Monica's packing at once.

"Are we going, then, this afternoon?"

"Yes, Miss Monica. Had you forgotten?"

Monica had not forgotten, but she had somehow felt certain that the catacylsm of the night before would alter everything. Surely, they could not leave London before she and Christopher had met again?

"Did mother say I might get up, Parsons?"

"No, Miss Monica. She hoped you'd rest in bed till she came up to you. I daresay she won't be very long now. It's getting on for twelve o'clock.'

It was, however, more than an hour later that Imogen Ingram sought her daughter.

She was much more composed, and also more disposed to severity than she had been the night before.

"No, you can't get up just yet, Monica. Anyhow, you look completely washed out. I shall send up a glass of port with your lunch, and you're to drink it. Never mind whether you like it or not. Now, darling, listen to me. I've spoken to

112

ather—and it's just as well I did, for almost directly afterwards I had a telephone call from a friend of mine—I'm not going to tell you who it was—and it seems that this story has got about already."

Mrs. Ingram paused, and swallowed hard, but it was evident that she had steeled herself against any further display of emotion.

"Father says, and I think he's quite right, that you're so young it may be quite possible for you to live it down, and it's a very, very good thing that we're leaving London immediately. People will have found something else to talk about before we bring you back to London. But, oh, Monica—when I think——!"

"Mother," said Monica desperately, "he wants to marry me—I know he does."

"Did he say so?"

"No—at least, not exactly."

"Either he did or he didn't. But he's not in a position to marry, even if he wanted to. I'm told that he has nothing at all, except his pay. It would be quite impossible, and a man who was a *gentleman* wouldn't dream of making love to a girl whom he couldn't afford to marry."

A dreadful feeling of despair invaded Monica.

This *couldn't* be the end of everything, surely.

She began to cry.

Her mother looked at her in compassion and perplexity mingled.

"Do you think yourself in love with him, my poor darling?"

Monica nodded vehemently.

"If only it hadn't happened like this—if only he'd been another *kind* of young man, perhaps it could somehow have been possible," said Mrs. Ingram. "Any husband is better than none at all, as I've always told you, and of course a girl who's been known to have any sort of adventure is very apt never to get any real chances. Men are so *terrified* of anything of that sort. How *could* you do it?"

Monica sobbed drearily.

"Don't go on crying like that. It's dreadfully bad for you and it will make your eyes so red."

"Must we go away to-day?"

"Indeed we must. Besides, what would be the object of staying on in London?"

Monica dared not answer that she thought she might see Christopher again, and wanted to do so more than anything else in the world. Instead she asked:

"Is father going to see—him?"

"No. He says much better not. It seems that his Regiment is likely to go out to India quite soon, and we shall take care, very good care, that he doesn't meet any of us again before then."

What a lot they had managed to find out, thought Monica drearily. It seemed impossible to her that she and Christopher Lane would not meet again, and at the bottom of her heart was still a hope that he, who loved her, would come to her, and put everything right.

"Now, darling, I needn't ask you to promise me that you will never, to anyone, say one word of this. Above all, not to Frederica and Cecily Marlowe. Their mother is a great friend of mine—I'm devoted to her—but she doesn't care *what* she says, so long as she has a good story to tell, and she knows everybody in London worth knowing. Our one hope is to let this die down of itself."

"Yes, mother."

"I'll talk to you again later. Rest a little while longer, darling, and you can get up after lunch and come down just before we start. We're leaving at three o'clock. Don't be afraid of meeting father—he's much upset, naturally, but he's quite ready to forgive you."

Monica returned her mother's kiss.

She felt dazed and wretched, and entirely drained of any initiative.

Presently her lunch was brought to her. On the tray lay an envelope addressed to herself.

She knew the handwriting and tore it open, breathless.

114

"Darling little Monica,

"I'm afraid I got you into trouble with your lady-mother last night. I'm so awfully sorry, and would have loved to help, but thought the best thing I could do was to clear out, as there really wasn't much explanation to offer, was there?!! Your friendship has been perfectly wonderful, and I shall never forget it—or you, needless to say. I do wish I'd had a chance of saying good-bye properly—just my luck that you should be leaving town just now.

"However, who knows when we may meet again, and meanwhile, don't forget me, and you may be sure that I shall often think of you and how sweet you've been to me.—Yours,

C.L.

"*P.S.* Do write sometimes."

Monica read the letter all through twice—the first time so quickly that she could hardly take in the meaning of the words, and the second time very slowly.

So it was quite true, and her mother had been right.

Christopher Lane was a cad. He hadn't, ever, really loved her and wanted to marry her. He'd just been taking advantage of a girl who had made herself cheap, and had allowed him to "take liberties" with her.

Before the tidal wave of pain and humiliation that had risen on the horizon of consciousness had actually broken, engulfing her youth and her confidence in herself and in life, Monica had time for that flash of astonished conviction:

Her mother had been right all the time.

It was a conviction from which she was never again wholly to free herself.

Imogen Ingram's despairing hope that no one need ever know of Monica's indiscretion was not wholly realized.

It was in vain that she invented variations of the true story: Monica had fallen in love with someone who could not afford to marry; Monica had broken off an engagement

115

with a very nice man whom she did not love *in that way*; Monica had been obliged to refuse someone whom she *did* love.

None of these explanations were whole-heartedly accepted as accounting for the dimming of Monica's prettiness, the quenching of her gaiety, and the new expression of anxiety that sprang now and then into her face.

Her second season was not a success. She began to be "difficult" and to say that she did not care about dancing. She made no new friends, and she ceased, altogether, to be attractive to men.

Book Two

The Anxious Years

CHAPTER I

WITH extraordinary rapidity time was slipping by. Monica was no longer a young girl in her first season. She was doing her second season, then her third—and then no one kept count any more. Imperceptibly, she joined the ranks of those whose "grown-up"-ness was taken for granted.

And nothing had happened.

She could not, herself, have told at what stage it was that the secret, gnawing anxiety, which soon never left her, first came into existence. The terrible affair of Christopher Lane did not seem to be directly responsible, heart-breaking and humiliating though it seemed at the time and for long afterwards. But when Monica came back to London after a summer spent in desperate attempts to conceal from everyone that anything was the matter, things seemed different.

It had proved impossible to keep her indiscretion entirely secret. Old friends had questioned Mrs. Ingram, Lady Margaret Miller's youngest daughter had told her mother of various conjectures, and Alice Ashe—as tactless as she was kind-hearted—had taxed Monica directly with having fallen in love, adding, with an obvious wish to console her, that poor Claude was perfectly miserable.

A landmark was reached on the day that Mrs. Ingram, just before Monica's twentieth birthday, said without preliminary:

"After all, poor Claude Ashe was very devoted to you, wasn't he? He might not be utterly impossible. . . ."

Two years earlier, Monica knew, her mother would not

have said, or felt, that Claude was anything but utterly impossible. That she should now view him in another light was the measure of her dismay, her gathering apprehension.

Claude Ashe still asked Monica for dances when they met in a ballroom, and he was once or twice invited to dinner in Eaton Square. Monica, however, knew with intuitive certainty that he was no longer attracted by her. Gradually she began to realize that the change was in herself, rather than in him. She was not, any longer, attractive.

The knowledge frightened her more and more.

It seemed impossible that she should be like Frederica and Cecily—one of those innumerable girls who would give anything to get married and never had the chance. Ever since she could remember Monica had heard of women, young or middle-aged, of whom that was said, half-contemptuously and half-compassionately. People had only ceased to say it of Frederica and Cecily because it was now taken for granted, and, moreover, their mother had given up taking them into Society, and allowed them to spend most of the time in the country with an old governess, with whom they still went for walks as they had done in their schoolroom days. Sometimes Monica went to stay with them; but she found the visits depressing, and her mother still said: "Visits of that kind are no real use. You don't meet anybody there, do you?"

"No," said Monica.

Meeting "anybody" meant unmarried young men.

One was taken to country houses in order to meet them. If none were provided, or if they were young men of whom nobody had ever heard before, Mrs. Ingram was indignant and felt that Monica had been invited on entirely false pretences. But gradually she was becoming less and less exacting. It seemed almost as though she would have welcomed Monica's engagement to anyone at all.

Her mother's anxiety and disappointment seemed to Monica harder to bear than almost anything. Sometimes Mrs. Ingram would look at her daughter, thinking herself

118

unobserved, with an expression of misery that was to Monica almost unendurable.

Gradually it came to be an understood thing between them that this continual preoccupation, that overshadowed the whole of life, must never be mentioned.

Even when Mrs. Ingram spoke of the engagements of other younger girls, or when Monica was asked to be a bridesmaid at Joan Miller's wedding, they displayed for one another's benefit a detached brightness that ignored everything below the surface.

"Young Culmstock is going to marry that tall girl— Mary Collier. He's one of the most eligible young men in London. I wonder how she did it."

"She's rather good-looking, isn't she?" said Monica with conscious generosity, for she had thought Mary Collier striking rather than good-looking.

"Oh no, darling," said her mother quickly. "I don't think so at all. She's much too tall for one thing. Well—she's brought this off, or her mother has for her. I see the wedding is to be quite soon. No wonder. They must be terrified of his shying off at the last minute."

Mrs. Ingram always assumed that any engagement must be a precarious affair, and that a man conferring so tremendous a benefit as marriage should be put beyond the possibility of changing his mind as quickly as possible.

Presently Monica found that most of the girls whom she had known in her first season had married. They were always very nice to her, and invited her to their houses, and talked cheerfully about its being her turn next, with only the faintest tinge of superiority.

Monica, in return, hinted gently that she had had an unhappy love affair, and was certain that she could never care for anybody else. She also implied that she had refused two or three proposals of marriage. She never felt really certain whether she was believed or not; and then one day she found that Mrs. Ingram was talking, lightly and yet very definitely, about her disappointment that Monica did not wish to marry.

119

"Of course, one doesn't want to say too much about it, but there have been one or two people that I should really have been *delighted* with—only Monica won't take them seriously. She says she doesn't care about men. Well, of course, some girls are like that."

A dreadful recollection of the contemptuous incredulity with which she had seen similar statements received from other mothers of unmarried daughters seared Monica through and through. Of *course* nobody believed those things any more than they believed vague assertions about a man who was *madly* in love with one, but couldn't afford to marry, or somebody who had gone abroad and asked one to "wait for him."

Such old, familiar subterfuges deceived nobody at all. If a girl reached the age of twenty-five and remained unmarried and was in no particular request, it was perfectly obvious that she and her mother had to say these things in order to try and save her face. But everybody knew, really, that she was a failure, and that men did not find her attractive.

Even the servants knew, thought Monica. Parsons, becoming a privileged person as time went on, would enquire, half wistfully and half with curiosity, when they were going to have a wedding in the house.

But after Monica's third season she made such references less often.

Vernon Ingram did not make them at all.

He had once, after the episode of Christopher Lane, spoken very seriously to Monica, and she never willingly allowed herself to remember that conversation. He had accused her of nothing at all excepting vulgarity, and Monica fully realized all that the word implied of censure and of shame.

She seldom thought of Christopher nowadays. The letter that she had received from him had destroyed the illusion of her ardent youth, and her infatuation had fallen dead with her self-confidence. She did not want to think of him, and was glad that he had gone abroad with his regiment and was no longer to be seen in London.

Monica was utterly dissatisfied and afraid to admit it, even to herself, when she met Carol Anderson at a wedding.

It was a secret misery now, to Monica, to attend a wedding, and she knew that her mother, too, suffered; but they always went, with a gallant pretence that there was no undercurrent of sick envy and mortification.

This time, it was the bridegroom's family by whom the Ingrams had been invited. They had never met the bride, but Monica had heard—with a quick sense of relief—that she was not a very young girl. Twenty-seven.

"Older even than I am. So perhaps——" thought Monica, standing beside her mother in church, and glad that her black fox furs and big black hat, tilted to one side of her head, suited her so well.

There were plenty of men, although most of them were probably married.

The bridegroom was bald, and not very interesting. It was said that he habitually drank a great deal too much, and Monica, since the announcement of the engagement, had heard surreptitious jokes as to the probability that he would arrive drunk for the wedding. The best man, people said, would have his work cut out.

Monica looked at the best man, standing decorous and frock-coated at the chancel rails. He was tall and good-looking, rather pale and serious, as though he were feeling more sense of responsibility than the bridegroom, who was red-faced and cheerful, and whispering behind his hand to his relations in the front bench. Monica barely gave him a glance.

She was concentrating her attention upon the best man, partly because she knew him to be unmarried and partly because she was attracted by his good looks.

At the reception afterwards he was introduced to her, and remained beside her for a length of time to which she was by now unaccustomed, for her great anxiety to please made her conversation forced and spasmodic.

Seen at close quarters Monica perceived that Carol Anderson was not quite as young and handsome as distance had led her to expect. There was something faintly theatrical about his good looks. He might possibly be about the same age as herself.

"*He might do*," was the message flashed by her subconscious mind, as they exchanged the commonplace observations proper to the occasion.

She liked his voice, and his rather plaintive smile, and heavy-lidded eyes of a tint between dark-hazel and grey.

They talked about weddings, and Anderson remarked that the traditional society wedding was in fact a relic of barbarism.

"Making so much fuss about something that in reality concerns only two people," he explained. "If a man and a woman do decide to live together, it seems to me a purely personal affair. They can make it a legal contract, if they want to, by going before the Registrar together."

"I'm afraid I like the idea of a church wedding," said Monica, smiling.

With some men, it was better to agree with everything they said, if they were to think one intelligent and responsive —but she knew instinctively that Carol Anderson would be more interested if she said what she really felt.

"Is that because you're religious, or because you like white satin and orange-blossom?"

"A little of both—but especially the white satin and orange-blossom, I think."

"Well, I don't blame you, because they'd be most becoming. And I hope you'll let me come and admire you when the time arrives."

"Wouldn't it be against your principles?" asked Monica with mock seriousness.

He replied in the same vein.

"There are some things—and people—for whom it's worth while to sacrifice one's principles."

"That's very nice of you. The least I can say in return is that I'll sacrifice mine, and come and witness your legal contract at the Registrar's office, when it takes place."

There was the faintest hint of an enquiry in her voice at the last words.

A curious change passed, for one instant, over Anderson's face. It was rather a withdrawal than a change of expression, and it was so fleeting that Monica wondered if she had not, perhaps, imagined it.

He answered almost immediately.

"That's charming of you. As a matter of fact, in my particular case, theories are not very likely to turn into practice. But I'll take the will for the deed, and be just as grateful to you."

"Don't you approve of marriage, then?"

"Very much," he returned, laughing. "Won't you have a glass of champagne?"

Monica accepted, and they raised their glasses to one another. A little thrill of excitement and pleasure went through her as their eyes met. She felt certain that he liked her.

The certainty was confirmed when Mrs. Ingram, joining Monica with the intention, evident to her daughter, of suggesting departure, as evidently changed her mind and smiled at Monica happily and confidently. Monica introduced Mr. Anderson.

"Do come and see us some time. We're always at home on Sunday afternoons," said Mrs. Ingram.

"I should like to so much. Next Sunday, if I may," declared the young man promptly.

Mrs. Ingram pretended to hesitate.

"Next Sunday—we're not going away this week-end, Monica, are we? No, that's all right. Then do come, Mr. Anderson. That'll be too delightful."

She turned away, and Monica knew, with the intuition peculiar to those who live together, that her mother was eagerly anxious not to break up her *tête-à-tête* with the young man.

But Carol Anderson, as best man, could not long remain talking to Monica, and in another moment he was called away.

She saw him again at the end of the afternoon, when the bride and bridegroom were saying good-bye to their friends. Most of the guests were crowding round the entrance of the hotel, preparing to wave enthusiastically when the car, already surreptitiously decorated with a satin slipper and a large horse-shoe, should drive off. Monica, standing on the pavement in Brook Street, smiling resolutely, suddenly caught sight of Mr. Anderson, looking taller than ever in his silk hat, hastening towards one of the foremost in the long line of waiting cars and carriages.

He paused as he passed her, then turned back.

"I'm dashing ahead, to look after them at Victoria, and all that. You never saw such a mountain of luggage!"

They laughed together.

"Good-bye. I shall look forward to seeing you next Sunday. You're in the book, I suppose?"

"Oh yes—I'm so glad you're coming."

He raised his hat, smiled at her, and was gone.

Neither Monica nor Mrs. Ingram made any reference to Carol Anderson as they drove home together half an hour later. They agreed that it had been a pretty wedding, and Mrs. Ingram made none of her usual criticisms on the bride and bridegroom. It was as though she felt that she could afford to be generous. The thought came to Monica quite involuntarily.

As they stood on their own doorstep whilst Mrs. Ingram searched her pocket, hidden in the folds of her skirt, for her latch-key, a large black cat sidled along the area railings, and then came up to them, pressing itself against the closed door.

Monica stooped to stroke its fur.

"Hullo, pussy—where have you come from?"

"Here it is——" Mrs. Ingram unlocked the door. "Don't let that cat——"

But the cat had already darted into the hall.

Monica laughed.

"I'll turn it out," she suggested.

To her surprise, her mother laid her hand on her arm.

"Never mind. Perhaps it's a good omen," she said seriously. "They say a black cat's lucky. It may be going to bring you luck, Monica."

With a sudden rush of compassion, mingled with quite unreasoning self-reproach, Monica realized imaginatively something of the piteous strain under which her mother lived. It must indeed be from some hidden depths of forlornness that Imogen Ingram, who was neither superstitious nor sentimental, could have so spoken!

They left the black cat undisturbed at the head of the stairs that led down to the servants' quarters in the basement.

That evening, and the day following, Monica was aware of a lightening in the atmosphere of the house. It was as though a new spirit of hopefulness was hovering on the threshold, not yet admitted, but seeking admittance.

On Saturday afternoon Mrs. Ingram, elaborately casual, enquired of her daughter whilst they sat at tea together in the drawing-room:

"Who was that young Anderson who was best man at the wedding the other day, darling? It just gave his name in *The Morning Post*, without saying if he was any relation or anything."

"I don't know, except that he's in the City. He told me so."

"Stockbroking, I suppose. Well, that might be all right," Mrs. Ingram said musingly, evidently speaking her thoughts aloud. "But you don't know *what* Andersons?"

"No, mother."

"Anderson might mean anything, of course."

There was a pause.

"Have you finished your tea, darling?"

"Yes, thank you."

"Then run down to the library, like a good girl, and bring me up *Burke*, will you?"

Monica obeyed without comment. Her mother became absorbed in the pages of the big red book. When she at last closed it, there was an air of faint satisfaction on her face.

"I thought so. He's one of the Gloucestershire Andersons. His mother must have been a Crawshay-Allen. The father is still alive: married a second time only a few years ago—a Miss Fowler—and lives at the place in Gloucestershire."

"Does it say if he's the only son?" Monica asked, her voice made carefully careless.

The faintest possible hesitation, preceding Mrs. Ingram's reply, warned Monica's abnormally sharpened perceptions that the answer was not altogether what she would have liked it to be.

"There's a child—a boy—by the second wife. Still—it might make no difference——"

Monica made no reply to the elliptical statement. It was not difficult to understand the implications that it carried, and she resented them the more bitterly because exactly the same train of thought had flashed through her own mind.

When she woke on Sunday morning, it was to the instant recollection that Carol Anderson had said he was coming that afternoon to Eaton Square.

Perhaps he wouldn't come, though, after all. Young men were not reliable. Monica strove to arm herself against the possibility of acute disappointment.

Neither she nor her mother made any reference whatever to the expected visitor.

The day followed its customary routine: church at St. Peter's in the morning, a walk across the Park—cold and unexhilarating in the raw chilliness of February—Sunday roast beef, apple-tart, Stilton cheese and celery, at home, and, soon afterwards, Vernon Ingram's announcement that he was going round to the Club.

"We're not expecting anyone, or going anywhere, this evening?" he enquired.

"No, dear. There's nothing."

"Then I shall try and get a rubber or two and perhaps dine at the Club."

His wife and daughter were not unaccustomed to such an announcement on Sundays. Mrs. Ingram always ordered a

126

cold supper that night, so that the servants might go to church, and there was a certain monotony about the weekly menu of cold beef, cold tart, and cold bundles of cheese-straws.

Monica often thought that her father's Club, where he could meet his friends, play cards, see all the latest illustrated papers, and order as varied a dinner as he chose, whatever the day of the week, must serve him as an agreeable refuge. She herself, of course, did not belong to a Club, and even had she done so, women's Clubs were usually uncomfortable and dingy, with badly cooked and served meals, and fires that refused to burn up.

At half-past three Mrs. Ingram, who had been leaning back in a corner of the sofa, with a Mudie novel open upon her lap, sat up very erect and said that Monica had better go and change her dress.

"In case anyone turns up."

"Won't this do?"

"No, darling. The collar is crumpled. Tell Parsons to wash it for you to-morrow morning—and the cuffs, too. And run upstairs and put on the green velveteen. It suits you."

Monica also thought that the green velveteen dress suited her, and felt grateful to her mother for having suggested it. She sighed with pretended reluctance and went upstairs.

It was cold in her bedroom, and Monica wished that she were allowed to have a fire there. There was always a fire in Mrs. Ingram's bedroom from four o'clock onwards, but she said that in Monica's case it was quite unnecessary, except in illness or very cold weather.

Monica unfastened her blue-serge dress, stepped out of it so as not to disturb her hair, and left it on the floor for the housemaid to put away. She went across to the wardrobe, shivering in her short-sleeved petticoat-bodice and silk under-skirt. The petticoat-bodice wouldn't do under the velveteen frock, which had a rather low-cut neck. It's bow of blue baby-ribbon had a way of appearing above the opening of her frock that compelled her to tuck it in again continually. Monica

127

decided that it was too cold to divest herself of anything at all, so after pinning down the recalcitrant blue bow, she put on a princess petticoat over all the rest, and then the green velveteen.

It certainly was a very pretty dress, and it was extraordinarily comfortable, as well as becoming, not to wear a high collar.

Monica looked at herself in the glass.

It occurred to her sometimes that she was not as pretty as she had been at eighteen. Her face was certainly paler and much thinner, and the loss of a tooth showed a gap when she smiled. But her hair was a satisfaction to her—brown and abundant, puffed out on either side of her head, and regularly and carefully waved at least once a fortnight.

This afternoon she was looking nice. The frock suited her, there was no sign of any spot on her chin, and her hair had "gone" successfully.

From far below, she thought she heard faintly the whirr of the front-door bell, for which she had, almost without knowing it, been listening all the afternoon. Monica kicked off her shoes and hastily pulled on a narrow, pointed pair of bronze ones with tiny gold beads on the toes, and went out to the landing.

Leaning over the banisters she could hear, distantly but unmistakably, the sound made by the baize-covered door at the head of the basement stairs, as it was pushed open.

Palter, going to open the door.

Monica rushed noiselessly down two flights of stairs, steadied herself outside the drawing-room and assumed an expression, then walked in quickly.

"Very nice, darling. Just catch up that piece of hair at the back—no, the other side—that's right. I think I heard the bell just a minute ago."

"Oh, did you?"

"It may very likely be poor cousin Blanche. She said she might come round."

It was cousin Blanche.

128

Monica, feeling acutely all her mother's disconcertment as well as her own, moved forward to receive the greeting of her ancient relative, whose sealskin coat always smelt faintly of camphor, reminding Monica invariably of her childhood.

Cousin Blanche never seemed to alter at all. She was now said, although a little uncertainly, to be nearly seventy; but Vernon Ingram, whose relation she was, always declared that she looked just as she had looked in his little boyhood—gaunt, aquiline, high-coloured, and with entirely unconvincing bright-brown hair closely curled round her head beneath the meshes of a net.

She had never married.

It was on that account, Monica had always taken for granted, that Mrs. Ingram invariably referred to her as "poor cousin Blanche," for cousin Blanche, in the literal sense of the term, was far from poor. She owned a house in Queen's Gate, and a box at the Opera, and some magnificent pearls, and she had quite recently bought a motor-car and engaged a chauffeur.

"Well, Imogen—well, Monica. You're looking very well, Monica. No, thanks, I'll keep my coat a little while, till I'm thawed. I should never be surprised if we had snow. How's Vernon?"

"Very well indeed, thank you, Blanche. He's not in just now, but I dare say presently—— Monica, give cousin Blanche a screen to hold in front of the fire."

They began to talk about relations. It was a topic that automatically arose in cousin Blanche's company. She was interested in all her relations, however distant, and always seemed to know what all of them were doing.

"You've heard about Sylvia, I suppose?"

Mrs. Ingram raised her eyebrows and glanced quickly at Monica, and then away again.

"Has it——?"

"She's got a little girl. Born yesterday morning."

"Is everything——?"

"Oh yes, quite, I believe. Her mother telephoned to me

last night. She said the baby was a lovely little thing, very healthy, weighed nearly eight pounds."

"I suppose they're very disappointed that it isn't a boy."

"Well, of course it's a disappointment, naturally, but Daisy said Sylvia was very sweet about it and said she didn't mind."

"I expect her husband had set his heart on its being a son."

"Naturally, they both hoped for a son, but after all—it's the first one, and they're young. Think of poor Adeline Ingram who had three daughters, one after another, and *then* twin girls."

"Dreadful, poor thing! Just imagine having to find husbands for them all!"

"That's what she says. She's most amusing about it—so brave of her I always think. She says she'll give them each a London season, one at a time, and the moment the eldest has had her chance, the second one comes out and the eldest one goes in again—and so on. But she's never going to be seen about with more than one daughter at a time."

"I don't blame her. It ruins a girl's chances to go about with two or three sisters. Men never know which is which, and besides, it's always such a bore for hostesses; they don't like to be unkind and only ask one sister, but of course nobody *wants* extra girls."

Monica was only partially attending to the conversation. She had heard similar conversations very often, and agreed in a tepid way with everything that had been said.

She was really thinking of little Sylvia, years younger than herself, who was safely married and had a baby. Monica was ashamed of herself for the furious jealousy that gnawed at her, and the secret, mean relief that at least Sylvia's triumph was only partial, since she had not achieved the supreme glory of giving birth to a boy. The door opened again: this time she had not heard the bell.

Palter announced sonorously:

"Mr. Pelham."

His frock-coat tightly fastened across increasing girth, his air of wooden impassivity scarcely disturbed by the slight,

130

grave smile that accompanied his handshake, Mr. Pelham sat down on a low chair beside the sofa, carefully drawing up his trousers at the knees as he did so.

He called on the Ingrams quite often, and had done so ever since Monica's first season. He could not possibly be thought interesting, and his rather clammy hands, the few streaks of dark hair brushed across his baldness, and his heavy paunch, made him slightly disagreeable to Monica. But she was, obscurely, grateful to him, because he still went to balls and could always be counted upon to ask her for a dance. She tried not to remember that the younger girls laughed at him behind his back, and asserted that he had been refused by half a dozen different heiresses.

This afternoon she was definitely glad to see Mr. Pelham. It would show cousin Blanche that men came to call. And if Carol Anderson *did* turn up. . . .

She tried to steel herself against disappointment by asserting inwardly that he would not come.

If she made herself believe that, perhaps she could cheat the fates. By five o'clock hope was sinking within her.

A taxi came down the quiet street and stopped outside.

Monica kept her eyes fixed upon Mr. Pelham, and repeated "Yes" and "I see" to all that he was painstakingly telling her about the Highlands.

She heard the slam of the street door.

Suspense was making her feel sick.

"Ring for some hot water, darling," said Mrs. Ingram.

"I think Palter's just coming, mother."

The butler threw open the door.

"Mr. Anderson."

The room, for an instant, reeled round Monica.

It was as from a distance that she heard her mother's exclamation: "How d'y do—this is very nice," uttered in a high, pleased, artificial voice.

CHAPTER II

IT DID not take long for Monica to make friends with Carol Anderson.

She found that he asked nothing better than to sit and talk to her for as long as she would listen, and after that first Sunday afternoon call he came often to Eaton Square.

Mrs. Ingram's early strictness, in the days when her daughter had first been grown-up, had long since relaxed, and when Mr. Anderson asked at the door for Miss Ingram, he was taken direct to Monica's sitting-room.

They sat, one on either side of the fire, and talked.

Almost at once he seemed to want to go below the surface of conversation and talk intimately.

Monica responded, deeply moved. She admitted to him that she had been lonely for years.

"I thought perhaps you had," he replied simply. "So have I."

Once or twice it seemed to her that he was hovering on the verge of a confidence, but she was so much afraid of risking any check to their friendship that she pretended unawareness. For the same reason, she dared not talk to him very much about herself.

"Men get very quickly bored with a woman who talks about herself," was one of Mrs. Ingram's axioms.

Not that she quoted it now, or gave Monica any advice at all. Only the daughter knew, as well as if she had been told so, that the mother was quivering with anxiety and with a hope that she hardly ventured to acknowledge, even to herself.

Perhaps—perhaps—*it* might be going to happen at last! Spring, coming early that year, seemed to waft new hope and happiness into the house in Eaton Square. Even Vernon

132

Ingram smiled proudly at Monica once or twice, and gave her one day an unexpected five-pound note, telling her to go and choose a pretty new hat for Easter.

Monica got the hat, and gloves, and a silk blouse as well. She wanted to wear them for an expedition that Carol Anderson had proposed.

He wanted her to drive with him into the country and spend an afternoon there. He had a motor-car. The day that they had chosen, towards the end of March, was a lovely one.

They went to Hindhead.

Monica, happier than she had been for years, knew that she was looking pretty, that Carol admired her, and that she need no longer feel inferior to other women. She was being sought out by a man, and not only that, but he was good-looking, tall, and a gentleman. It seemed too good to be true.

They left the car at the big new hotel after lunch, saying that they would return for tea, and began to walk down the long hill, branching off presently on to common land.

"Isn't it wonderful?" said Carol suddenly. He looked round at her, smiling. "The day, I mean, and having this weather, and knowing you, and everything."

Monica's heart leapt.

"I feel like that too."

"Should you be cold if we sat down for a little while?"

"Not a bit. It's so mild—and besides I've got quite warm walking."

Monica really hardly knew what she was saying, but there were a number of felled trees lying by the side of a deep ditch, and she took her seat upon one of them. Carol sat beside her.

She glanced at his profile, motionless beside her. He was poking little holes in the ground with his stick. At last he spoke.

"Do you remember the first time we met, at the Lester wedding? It seems queer, to think it was only about two months ago."

"Yes, doesn't it. I feel as if I'd known you so much longer than that."

"I've sometimes wondered whether——"

He broke off abruptly, then began again.

"Look here, I've been meaning to ask you whether you won't call me Carol, instead of Mr. Anderson. It seems rather absurd, to be so conventional, after all. And may I call you Monica?"

"Yes, of course."

"Thanks awfully." For the first time, he turned his head and looked at her, smiling rather shyly.

"Because we are friends—Monica."

A small shiver of excitement passed through her when she heard him speak her name.

"I feel that too."

She wanted to say much more—to tell him that she cared deeply for his friendship, that she wanted him to tell her everything about himself, and to give him her confidence in return—but she was inhibited by her own emotion, her abiding sense of insecurity, and the ever-present recollection of her mother's reiterated warnings—that to show a man how much one liked him, was to cheapen oneself in his estimation. She dared not risk it.

"The very first time I saw you, at the wedding, I wondered if I should ever get to know you. To know you really well, I mean."

"Did you—Carol?"

He gave her a quick glance and smile, in recognition of her use of his name.

"I was most dreadfully unhappy that day, and I would have given anything in the world to know that there was someone I could talk to—someone who'd understand."

"Tell me why you were unhappy."

"I've never told anyone," said Carol slowly. "But I think I'd like to tell you."

" I wish you would," Monica said, sincerely and earnestly.

She felt that his confidence would be almost a pledge of another, more profound, relation between them.

Presently he began to speak, at first slowly and with hesitation, but afterwards more freely.

"I didn't want to be best man at that wedding—or at any wedding. You see—the only woman I've ever cared for is married to Lester's brother."

Monica caught her breath.

Two thoughts sprang, almost simultaneously, to life within her.

He cares for somebody else.

But she's married.

Anderson went on speaking, looking down at the little dents that he was still assiduously making with the point of his stick.

"Do you remember talking about weddings that day, and I said they oughtn't to be church affairs at all, but just a contract, civil if they liked, between two people?"

"Yes, I remember."

"Viola Lester is married to a brute—she's been tied to him for seven years—and she won't divorce him or leave him because she's a religious woman," said Carol bitterly.

"Did you—want her to leave him?"

"Yes, I did."

He squared his shoulders and then turned and looked at her. There was something faintly histrionic in the gesture.

"Yes, I did. You're not shocked, are you, Monica?"

"No, I'm not shocked," Monica repeated dully. And after a moment she added:

"Tell me about it."

"There isn't much to tell, really. I met her two years ago and fell in love with her. I'd had fancies—one or two—and thought myself in love before. But this was quite different. It was something absolutely real."

He spoke with an intensity of conviction that seemed to require acknowledgement.

Monica said: "I know."

"I saw she was very unhappy. Her husband drinks, and does other things as well—she was only nineteen when she

135

married him. That her people should have let her do such a thing——" He spoke through clenched teeth.

A strange, dreamy feeling as though she had heard all this before began to creep over Monica. She did not understand nor attempt to analyse it.

"At first we were just friends. I tried to make things a little easier for her—I hope perhaps I did—I was able to help her over business once or twice. And we used to talk. I hope —in fact, I *know*"—he spoke now with quiet confidence, "that she was less lonely after I had come into her life. But I don't think she really took me seriously until—one night in June. It was the tenth of June. I don't suppose that I shall ever forget that date however long I may live."

Carol paused and let the walking-stick drop from his hand. When he spoke again his voice had taken on a deep, restrained tone.

"I couldn't stand it any longer. I asked her to let me take her away. I told her that I—loved her."

His face had flushed darkly, and he was bending and twisting with both hands a stout branch that had lain on the ground at their feet.

"There were no children. If she'd had children, it would have been different. I realize *absolutely* what a woman feels about her children—I have a peculiarly strong imagination, much more so than most men, and I understand women. But there was nothing like that to hold her. Only this—this so-called religion. I don't mean that she wasn't absolutely sincere, of course—she was only too much so. But to me it's so incredible—so utterly monstrous—that anyone should think that God requires a woman to stay with a man she loathes, and who makes her wretched."

"Did she care for you too?" asked Monica.

He hesitated before replying, but at last said:

"She would never, actually, admit it. But—yes, I think she did." His voice gained in assurance. "I know she did. I understood her in some ways much better than she understood herself. I know perfectly well that I was the right man for her. I could have made her happy. She knew it, too, at the bottom of her heart. Only she wouldn't own to it. That sounds as if I'm blaming her—and I couldn't do that."

The branch snapped between his fingers, and he continued to break it, rather violently, into small pieces as he went on speaking.

"I can't even begin to tell you how much I cared for Viola —and still care."

Monica's heart sank, and she experienced a fierce resentment against herself. Was she, then, incapable of a generous and self-forgetful response? Carol Anderson was honouring her with his deepest confidence—one that he said he had never bestowed upon anybody else. She could not, and would not, fail him.

"Two weeks before Jack Lester's wedding, I'd seen Viola, and asked her if she'd come away with me. I thought she was nearer saying Yes than she'd ever been before. I let myself hope. I was a fool, I suppose. I'm not a very hopeful person, as a rule. Perhaps I'm rather more free from illusions than most men—I don't know. Anyhow, I thought I'd won Viola. And then—then, Monica——"

The last available fragment of the stick snapped, and was flung away. Carol Anderson hid his face in his hands.

"It's no good. I can't tell you. It goes too deep. Forgive me, please, Monica. You've been a perfect dear to me. But I can't talk—not even to you. I'm not made that way."

Monica, not knowing what to say, rather timidly laid her hand upon his. It was taken and grasped tightly.

"Thank you for listening to me."

"Won't you tell me the rest, Carol?"

"There's not anything to tell, really. She wrote to me and said that it must come to an end. She was going abroad with her husband. He was ill, and she was going to forgive him, and let him start again. They—they're going round the world. They'll be away two years, or more."

"She'll come back," hazarded Monica.

"Perhaps. But it's over. I know Viola. She means what she says. If she's promised to give him another chance, she'll do it, and stick to it. The only thing that I can do now, is to do as she asked, and never go near her again."

"Carol—I'm so sorry."

"Thank you, my dear." He achieved a difficult smile. "Well, now you know my story. It's not a very unusual one, I dare say. And yet——" he seemed to recollect himself, "it *is* unusual, I suppose. Most men have something of the kind in their lives, I dare say—but they don't take it as hard as I do. My capacity for suffering is an absolutely extraordinary one. I do know that for a fact."

"Some day——"

He shook his head.

"No. If you mean that some day I shall mind less about this, you're wrong. It will always be exactly the same to me. I'm like that."

Monica felt that he did not wish either to be reasoned with or contradicted on the point.

She said nothing.

"Of course, I'm going on with everyday life just as usual. My going to that wedding, as best man, proves that. I *know* that I have a tremendously strong will, and I've put every ounce of it into preventing anybody's knowing what I feel— except you, Monica."

His smile at her, and deep look straight into her eyes, moved her emotionally, in spite of the dead, cold weight of disappointment at her heart.

"Please always go on telling me things, Carol. I want you to, and I understand."

"I know you do. And it's been a relief to talk to you. If I don't do it again for a long while—perhaps for years—you mustn't mind, or think it's because you're less my friend. It's only that I'm a person who is naturally very reserved— to whom speech doesn't come at all easily."

Carol Anderson passed his hand across his eyes, as though clearing from them the mists of some inner preoccupation.

He looked down at the broken fragments of the branch lying all round him.

"Did I do that? How destructive!"

Smiling ruefully, he bent and picked up his own walking-stick once more.

"It's grown chilly, hasn't it?"

Monica had felt that it had for some while. The sun had gone behind a bank of cloud, and they had been sitting on the log a long time. She was cold and cramped when Carol gave her his hand and pulled her up from her low seat.

When they were both on their feet, he still retained her hand for a moment.

"This has been wonderful, Monica. I never thought that I should find anybody like you."

Words that might, and should, have been used if he had been in love with her, she thought drearily.

It was something to have his friendship, perhaps. It would make life less lonely.

Quite involuntarily that thought was immediately followed by another one—the echo of Imogen Ingram's voice:

"Never be silly enough to let a man talk to you about being *friends* with him. There's no such thing as friendship between a man and a woman. That kind of thing leads to nothing. . . ."

The only thing that mattered was to get married, and now it seemed unlikely that Carol Anderson would ever ask her to marry him after all. He was all the time thinking about somebody else.

She was able to feel intensely sorry for him, partly because she was more attracted by him physically than she was willing to admit, and partly because of his own intense belief in the reality and immensity of his suffering. It carried conviction, whilst she was with him.

They walked some way further before turning back to the hotel, and Carol earned Monica's fervent gratitude because, very gently and affectionately, he led her on to tell him the story of her youthful love-affair with Christopher Lane.

She had long ago evolved a formula that salved her hurt self-respect. By now she had come to believe in it herself. "There was somebody that I cared for, once. He cared for me too—but only for a little while, and not as much as—as I thought he did. It was marvellous while it lasted."

Her eyes grew misty as she tried, vainly, to recapture something of the glamour and excitement that had surrounded her brief, youthful romance. It seemed, actually, to have happened to someone else, for she could no longer revive in herself any spark of the innocent, ignorant confidence in the right of youth to love and happiness that had been hers at the age of eighteen.

"So you've known what it is to care for someone too, Monica?"

"Yes. In a way, I shall always care for him. It's on that account, really, that I haven't ever been able to care for anybody else."

Monica believed, at least partially, in the truth of what she was saying. Her life would have been so utterly unendurable had she not been able to believe something of the kind, that this legend of her own fidelity had crystallized within her by imperceptible degrees, and had become part of the fabric of existence. She offered it to Carol Anderson without any sense of being other than wholly sincere.

"Sometimes," she said, "I think that I shall never marry."

Anxiously, she waited for his reassurance.

"Some people can accept the second-best. I don't think you could, any more than I could. I know perfectly well, for instance, that I shall never marry, because I can never care for any other woman as I cared—*care*," he corrected himself, "for Viola Lester."

"Everyone isn't like that."

"No, though I think women are more often than men. I suppose I'm exceptional in that sort of way."

"I think you are," said Monica.

She knew that was what he wanted her to say, and it would

140

have been impossible to Monica to risk losing his evident confidence in her sympathy. Far below the regions of conscious thought was the hope that from friendship and sympathy might spring sexual desire.

She was the more deeply unaware of this because of the weight of bitter disappointment that had descended upon her ever since Carol had said that he loved another woman. All through the drive home, she could feel that knowledge waiting to crush the newly born hope that had seemed so fair only that morning. Worst of all, she almost felt, would be the moment when she would have to let her mother know—casually, and as though it mattered not at all to either of them—that Carol Anderson was, after all, "no real use."

They did not talk very much on the way home. As they neared Eaton Square Carol said to her:

"I know that what I've said is absolutely safe with you. I don't mean to say that no one else knows about it, because, naturally, it was more or less inevitable that one or two people should have guessed. Not from me, as a matter of fact. I have the most extraordinary powers of self-command, curiously enough. A great many people have told me that, and I know it's true. But I couldn't bear anyone ever to know that I'd spoken about it. I never have, except to you."

"You're not sorry that you did, Carol?"

"No. You've been perfectly wonderful to me, and—it's helped, telling you about it. I do want to see a lot of you, Monica, if I may."

"Yes, I'd like it," she said faintly.

The words were true enough, but she reflected bitterly how differently she would have felt them, twenty-four hours earlier.

At the door she asked Carol to come in, but was relieved when he thanked her and refused.

"I want to see you again though, very soon. May I come round to-morrow—about six o'clock?"

"Yes, do," said Monica.

She was glad, after all, that he wanted to come.

He liked her so much—she felt certain of that—might he not come to find her indispensable?

It was a forlorn hope enough—but it was a hope.

As Monica went wearily up the family stairs she met her mother coming down.

Mrs. Ingram wore more than her usual aspect of brightness. There was a kind of expectancy in the smile and exclamation with which she greeted Monica.

"Have you had a nice day, darling?"

"Lovely, thank you."

Monica had known that she could not altogether deceive her mother. They had lived together too long, and Monica had been forced into too close an intimacy, all through her early years, for reticences or evasions to avail her now.

The reflection of the disappointment that she tried hard to keep out of her voice was instantly visible in Mrs. Ingram's expression, although she continued to smile, and said: "I'm so glad, darling. I expect you're tired."

"I am, a little."

"Why not lie down and rest a little before dressing? You haven't forgotten that we're dining out to-night?"

"No. I think I will rest a little, first."

"I should. You didn't bring Mr. Anderson in, then?"

"He asked if he might come," rejoined Monica quickly, knowing that it would comfort her mother to hear that, in the mysterious chill that had descended upon their hopes.

"He brought me to the door of course, and asked if he could come in, but I thought it would make rather a rush, as we're going out, and he's coming to-morrow instead."

She averted her eyes from the wave of relief that she knew was passing over her mother's face.

"Quite right, darling. You've had a long day. And besides——" Mrs. Ingram left the sentence unfinished, but Monica knew what she meant.

"*Besides, it's much wiser not to let a man think that he has only to ask. . . .*"

She went into her own room.

Incredibly soon, the mechanism of Monica's consciousness adjusted itself to her new awareness of Carol Anderson's emotional pre-occupation with another woman. She found not only consolation but grounds for hope in his dependence upon the sympathy that she gave him without stint.

It was a relief to her when, a few days after the drive to Hindhead, her mother, with some hesitation, told her that she had heard, from a connection of the Lesters, that Carol Anderson was said to have been very much in love with an unhappily married woman.

"I know," said Monica calmly.

"Is it absolutely all over, then?" her mother asked eagerly.

"In a way I think it is. I mean—the woman was Mrs. Felix Lester, wasn't she?"

"Yes."

"Hasn't she gone abroad with her husband for two years?"

"Yes, I believe she has. Of course, darling, I don't want you to betray any confidences." Mrs. Ingram paused rather wistfully but Monica made no sign, afraid of betraying Carol who had said that he should not like anyone to know that he had spoken about his love for Viola.

"Naturally, one rather wondered. . . . But after all, many a man has been caught on the rebound."

It was exactly what Monica had thought, at the back of her mind, but it shocked her disagreeably to hear the thought put into words, accustomed though she was to the enunciation of Mrs. Ingram's creed.

"A young man's infatuation for a married woman means very little, really. And, in a way, it's much *safer* than—anything else. There's no question of marrying, or anything like that. He's absolutely free. And when a man is fresh from a disappointment of that kind, it very often means that he's much readier to think of settling down than he might be at any other time."

It was evident that Mrs. Ingram believed, and wanted Monica to believe, that there was still hope.

143

Monica very often, through the spring and summer, was able to persuade herself that there was still hope.

She saw Carol almost daily; he wrote to her sometimes and telephoned often.

He liked to be alone with her, and always he talked to her about himself, or about himself and Viola Lester. Monica pitied him, and believed his assurances that he had never bestowed his confidence upon anybody else. It was a long while before she even admitted to herself that his plaintive gratitude and affection could not wholly atone for his egotism, his endless dramatizations of himself, and his un-wearying self-pity.

Their friendship was not constructive. Carol, she realized by degrees, was instinctively averse from anything that might tend to destroy his conception of himself. He had no real wish to be consoled, or to allow himself to recover from his un-happiness. Actually, he quietly fostered and nursed it, unwilling to relinquish that which made him interesting in his own eyes.

Monica did not closely analyse Carol Anderson, but she felt, by degrees, that she understood him. She was fond of him because he was affectionate and grateful and had a certain child-like charm of manner towards women, and because he was the person with whom she had most nearly, in her life, achieved intimacy.

Underneath everything persisted her dogged, desperate wish that he should some day ask her to marry him.

CHAPTER III

"THE Marlowes are going to be in London next week," exclaimed Monica, surprised.

"Fricky and Cecily—poor things!—are they really? I thought their mother had practically given up having them in town."

"It's more than two years since they were last in Belgrave Square," Monica admitted. "They both say they like the country better."

"Girls have to say *something*, darling, when they get to that age. Even Cecily must be getting on now. I can't think why their mother doesn't let them travel—send them round the world, or something like that. She could perfectly well afford it, and she might get one of them off her hands at last. Supposing Cecily married—I always think she's the less impossible of the two—it would probably be someone living abroad, and then she could have Fricky to stay, and very likely find someone for her as well."

"I can't imagine what Frederica would do if Cecily married."

"What does it matter *what* she'd do?" enquired Mrs. Ingram calmly. "The only thing that matters is that one of them should find a husband. Not that I suppose there's much hope now, really."

The familiar sense of misery welled up in Monica, as she heard the words, and it was evident that a similar train of thought had been roused in her mother.

She said:

"Ask them to lunch or something, poor things. Of course, all their contemporaries are married, I should imagine— they must be years older than you are."

145

Monica made no reply.

"I'm sorry for poor Theodora Marlowe," said Mrs. Ingram. "Not that I think she's been a particularly good mother—I don't—but it's very hard on her that both those girls should be so completely unattractive. They're not bad-looking, either of them, and there's plenty of money—and yet look at them! Not a single serious chance, I don't believe —not one!"

"I think it would be much better," said Monica boldly, "if they went and *did* something. Work, of some kind."

Mrs. Ingram shook her head.

"I don't see how it would be possible," she said not un-reasonably. "There's only nursing, or teaching, for that sort of girl, and both are hard work. They've never been trained to do anything at all. I'm sure they'd break down in a week."

Monica was sure of it too.

"Settlement work," she suggested.

"Well, I suppose so. There's always that kind of thing— good works, and so on. Everybody knows what it means— that a girl hasn't been able to find a husband, and is bored with living at home and doing nothing."

And looking at her daughter, Mrs. Ingram added quickly:

"It would break my heart, Monica, if *you* ever wanted to go in for anything of that kind."

Monica knew too well that the words were, at least meta-phorically, true.

Carol Anderson still came to see her often, and his liking for her, after nearly a year of friendship, seemed to have varied not at all. He still talked to her of his undiminished love for Viola Lester, and still sought to persuade himself and her that time could never, in his case, bring its customary alleviations. Monica did not feel him to be consciously in-sincere: it was rather as though he had succeeded in hypno-tising himself into believing in the existence of a romantic figure, called by his own name. He would admit nothing that interfered with his creation.

Every time that Monica realized this, she realized, too,

146

that Carol Anderson would never ask her to marry him. If he ever did marry, his wife must be a woman who could honestly subscribe to his visions of himself as a Great Romantic. Side by side with these inescapable certainties was Monica's unrecognized intention of letting Frederica and Cecily Marlowe see Carol Anderson as a man devoted to herself, whom she could marry as soon as she desired so to do.

Two days after their arrival in London she went to see them. They looked paler, more listless and dejected than ever. Frederica's tyranny over her sister seemed to have gained in strength, but now even Cecily occasionally offered to it a faint resistance. It was almost the only sign of initiative shown by either.

"Are you staying long?" Monica enquired.

"We don't know," Cecily explained, like a child. "Mother hasn't said yet. She's in bed with a chill at the moment."

"Cecily isn't going near her for fear it should be influenza," Frederica thrust in quickly.

"She doesn't want either of us. I hope she'll be all right by to-morrow. Tell us about you, Monica."

"There isn't anything much to tell."

The other two stared at her in unspoken enquiry.

"I'm having quite a good time," said Monica desperately. "I've got a new friend, by the way. I want you to meet him. A man called Carol Anderson—one of the Gloucestershire Andersons."

"Oh, Monica! Is he going to be any use?" asked Cecily.

Monica pretended to hesitate.

"I don't quite know. I can't make up my mind."

"Do say what he's like. How old is he?"

"About the same age as I am."

"That needn't matter, really."

"No. I know."

"Is he tall?"

"Yes, very. Just over six foot," said Monica triumphantly.

"My dear! Then he *must* be poor, or frightfully hideous or something."

"He's quite fairly well off, I believe. He's in the City. And he's very good-looking."

"Monica! Has he asked you yet?"

Monica shook her head.

"Not exactly."

She saw immediately from Frederica's expression that the admission discredited everything that had gone before.

"One can always tell," she said proudly. "And I don't at all want him to say anything, till I'm sure."

"But, Monica," cried Cecily, "surely you wouldn't hesitate for a minute? There are so awfully few men to go round, *any* husband would be better than none—and he sounds so splendid." And she added piteously: "We can't all three be failures."

"Don't," said Frederica, frowning. "You talk as if marriage was the only thing that can make women happy. But there are lots of unhappy married women."

"They aren't unhappy in the same way. And people don't *despise* them, anyway," said Cecily simply.

The three looked at one another.

"If even *one* of us could get a husband, it wouldn't be so bad," said Cecily suddenly. "I mean, Fricky and I. You'll get married, I expect, Monica, one of these days."

"I don't want a husband. I hate men," Frederica observed sullenly.

Neither of the other two made any pretence at believing her.

"Why can't one have a career, or even work, like a man?" Monica asked helplessly. "I know everybody would say that it was because we hadn't been able to get married—but they'll say that anyway."

"There isn't any work for girls of our kind," Frederica asserted. "Not any that we should be allowed to do. The only way is to become religious, and go and do some kind of good works, with a whole crowd of old maids and people who don't belong to one's own class."

"There are causes and things," said Cecily timidly.

Frederica laughed disagreeably.

"Yes, the militant suffragettes, I suppose you're thinking of. Women who bite policemen, and kick and fight in the streets."

"Besides," said Monica, "it's such nonsense about the vote. What does it matter whether women have it or not? They don't really care themselves, I don't suppose. It's just hysteria, and wanting to be conspicuous, that makes them go on like that."

She was repeating in all good faith, without either reflection or knowledge behind it, exactly what she had heard said by Vernon and Imogen Ingram, and the majority of their contemporaries. Frederica, who could not bear to admit that anything from which she was herself debarred had value, supported her vehemently.

Cecily said nothing. Of the three, she was the most nearly capable of thinking for herself independently and without personal bias, and only her secret terror of Frederica's overbearing protectiveness, that would gladly have pinned her down into an eternal babyhood, kept her silent.

"It would be different, I suppose, if one had some special talent. Being able to write or draw or something like that. Plenty of girls go to the Slade School of Art."

"Their people don't like it though, as a rule," said Frederica. "They always hope the girl'll marry in the end—and of course she usually does. I wouldn't mind, if only there was something to *do*."

"Wouldn't Lady Marlowe let you do anything?"

"I dare say she might, but what is there?" asked Frederica helplessly. "There isn't anything I *could* do."

It was, as Monica knew, perfectly true. There was nothing whatever that she, or Frederica, or Cecily, could do with any particular efficiency.

They had been brought up with no end in view except that of marriage: and they had not married.

There was a certain relief, Monica felt, in talking more frankly than they had done yet—for she knew instinctively that neither Cecily nor Frederica had entirely accepted the view presented to them of Carol Anderson as a potential husband for herself.

They parted with a promise to meet again in a few days.

On the following afternoon Frederica telephoned to Monica.

Her voice sounded sharp and frightened.

"Mamma is much worse, Monica. Will you ask your mother who is a good doctor? Ours is out of London, and I think someone ought to see her at once."

"Oh Fricky—I'm so sorry. What is it? Influenza? Yes, of course, I'll give you our own doctor's telephone number at once. Is there anything we can do?"

Monica searched through the little morocco book that held the exchange numbers most often in use, and found what she wanted.

"Thank you," said Frederica's breathless voice.

"Can I do anything, Fricky?"

"I don't know. Perhaps—perhaps you could come and take Cecily away if mamma isn't better to-morrow. You know how delicate she is, and I'm so afraid of her catching anything."

Monica felt a spasm of impatience. Frederica's obsession was as strong as ever, and every year made it more ridiculous.

"But Fricky——" However, what was the use of saying anything? She turned it into: "Do you know what the matter is with Lady Marlowe? Is it influenza? Has she got a temperature?"

"She's a hundred and one, Rouse says. Rouse thinks it's influenza. Good-bye, Monica. I'll ring up again this evening."

"Good-bye," repeated Monica.

It was evident that Rouse, Lady Marlowe's elderly maid, was in charge of the invalid. Monica admitted to herself that it was impossible to imagine being nursed by either Frederica or Cecily.

At seven o'clock the telephone-bell rang again.

"This is Frederica speaking. Your doctor sent his partner —he says mamma has a sharp attack of influenza, and he's sending in a hospital nurse to-night."

"I'm so sorry. Is she very bad?"

Monica, like Frederica, was completely ignorant of most of the laws governing health and sickness.

"Dr. Corderey says we're not to worry. He's coming again to-morrow morning of course."

"I wish you could have had our old Dr. Bruce. He's so nice."

"This one's nice, too. He's quite young, but I should think he's a very good doctor. Mamma liked him."

"Are you looking after her, Fricky?"

"Part of the time, with Rouse—till the nurse comes."

"Don't catch influenza. May I come round to-morrow morning?"

"Yes, please do."

"Mother sent you her love, and was so sorry to hear about your mother, and you're to be sure and let me know if there's anything we can do to help."

"Thanks so much, Monica. Please thank your mother from me. I must go now. Good-bye."

Frederica's voice had sounded slightly important, as though she felt herself to be busy, and in request. Monica thought that she could understand it, if the feeling brought relief, and a certain measure of pleasant excitement. She wondered whether Cecily was permitted to have any share in it.

The next day she walked round to Belgrave Square, with her mother, to make enquiries and to leave a sheaf of roses.

They found Cecily in the big drawing-room, looking wan and exhausted, almost as though she might be ill herself.

"Mamma is rather better, thank you," she said politely, after thanking Mrs. Ingram for the roses. "Her temperature was down this morning and she had quite a comfortable night. The doctor is with her now."

"Where is Frederica? She's not caught influenza, I hope?" enquired Mrs. Ingram.

Cecily's pale face grew scarlet. She had a child's tendency towards violent changes of colour.

"She's with the doctor, upstairs in mamma's room. She'll be down in a few minutes."

Monica guessed that Frederica had succeeded in obtaining from her mother or the doctor a prohibition to Cecily against entering the sick-room, and that Cecily deeply and passionately resented it, but had not the courage either to disobey or to complain to anyone else of Frederica's tyranny.

"You don't look very well yourself, dear," said Mrs. Ingram good-naturedly. "Why not come round to us for a day or two, till mamma is better again? We should be delighted to have you."

Cecily flushed again, and hesitated.

"Thank you very much," she said at last. "It's very kind of you. But I'm not sure if I ought to. You see, influenza is very catching, isn't it, and supposing Fricky gets it from mamma. . . ."

Good heavens, thought Monica impatiently, what a vicious circle it was! Had Cecily begun to develop her sister's insane obsession of anxiety?

She glanced at her mother. She knew, without thinking about it, that Mrs. Ingram would not take Cecily's protest at all seriously, partly because, in a quite kind and impersonal way, she despised Cecily completely, and partly because it was perfectly well known, to all three of them, that the real decision would not lie in Cecily's hands at all.

"Perhaps we'd better see what your mother thinks——" Mrs. Ingram was beginning, when Frederica came into the room with Dr. Corderey.

At the sight of the visitors she looked disconcerted, as she always did when taken unawares, and began a nervous and incoherent attempt at introduction.

"Dr. Corderey and I have met before," said Mrs. Ingram briskly. "Monica, this is Dr. Bruce's partner, Dr. Corderey. I hope your patient is better?"

"Yes, on the whole, thank you. But influenza is a treacherous thing, and Lady Marlowe has had a very sharp turn. She'll have to be very careful for a few days."

152

"So many people try and get up too soon, after influenza, I always think," said Mrs. Ingram.

They were all standing, and there was a certain constraint in the atmosphere.

Mrs. Ingram, whose social code was entirely inelastic, had a special manner for members of the professional classes, some degrees less cordial than that reserved by her for the working classes proper.

She had known the elderly Dr. Bruce for many years, and with him was often quite natural and friendly, although it would not have seemed to her possible to invite him to dine at her house—but Dr. Corderey was much younger than Dr. Bruce—probably not yet forty—she had only met him once before, and it was impossible to be certain that he might not "take advantage" of the opportunity.

Thus Monica, guided by intimate and prolonged experience of her mother's mental processes, interpreted Mrs. Ingram's politely patronizing tones, and evident determination to remain standing and thereby oblige Dr. Corderey to do the same.

Monica looked at him.

He was a dark, square, youngish-looking man, short and stocky, with a serious, clean-shaven face, and a pair of very intelligent, brilliant dark eyes.

He had given Monica a very comprehensive look on being introduced, and now he was turning exactly the same attentive, alert gaze on Cecily Marlowe, without speaking.

"I've been suggesting that Cecily should pay us a visit for a few days, Frederica, if she's to be kept away from your mother's room. It will be less lonely for her," said Mrs. Ingram.

"Oh, thank you. I think that's a very good idea," Frederica said eagerly.

Monica looked at her rather indignantly. Really, Cecily was a little fool to stand this sort of thing from a sister barely three years her senior. Why didn't she answer for herself?

Surprisingly, Cecily did so.

"It's very kind of Mrs. Ingram, but I'd rather not go just now," she said in a voice that betrayed her labouring breath. "I think that while mamma is ill, I ought to be here just as much as Frederica."

In an instant, the atmosphere had become tense. The point at issue might be trivial: the morbid emotional values surrounding it were exaggerated out of all proportion.

Even Mrs. Ingram seemed momentarily perplexed.

"But my dear child——" she began, and stopped.

"Cecily!" said Frederica. Her look at her sister was one of mingled command, entreaty, and bitter reproachfulness.

Cecily had turned white. The familiar dents came and went, at the corners of her nostrils.

The masculine voice of the strange doctor cut across the secret, subtle entanglements of the moment.

"For the present," he said briskly, "I don't want anybody from this house to go and stay anywhere else. There's always a faint risk of carrying the germ to another household, and that would be a pity."

"But my sister hasn't been near infection," said Frederica quickly.

"You can't tell that," he returned. "In any case, it's wiser to take no chances."

Turning to Cecily he smiled for the first time, showing beautiful teeth.

"As your medical man, I desire you to remain where you are for the present," he said decisively.

"Yes, thank you," faltered Cecily absurdly.

She was grasping the back of a chair, and her eyes looked scared and enormous in her white face.

Mrs. Ingram was not pleased. Her raised eyebrows and closely compressed lips told Monica so plainly.

"We can talk about it another time," she said, with an assumed lightness that was not intended to deceive anybody. "I dare say mamma will be packing you both back to the country again in a few days, if there's much of this influenza about."

154

"There is," said the doctor. "A great deal of it. Now I'll just write out that prescription, if I may."

He moved without embarrassment across to the writing-table, and sat down.

"Have you got a good nurse?" Mrs. Ingram made conversation to Frederica.

"Yes, very, I think."

"They *can* be thoroughly tiresome, and give a lot of trouble."

"This one seems quite nice."

"Well, I'm glad to hear it. If she gets on with the servants all right it'll be a great mercy. They don't as a rule. But I suppose Rouse can manage that all right."

It was evident that Mrs. Ingram did not think that Frederica could manage that, or anything else.

Nor did she.

Going home with Monica, a few minutes later, she impatiently said as much.

"Really, those two girls aren't normal. I sometimes think they're neither of them quite all there. The simplest thing upsets them—and nobody knows why. I don't suppose they know themselves."

"They've always been like that," said Monica helplessly.

"No, they haven't," her mother contradicted her sharply. "Morbid and silly, I agree, they've always been—more or less—but not to this extent. If they'd married, either or both of them, they'd probably be all right. It's having nothing to do, and nothing to think about, except themselves and their own feelings, that makes them react on one another to such an extent. Cecily looks to me as if she might go off her head at any minute."

"Mother, you don't mean *really*?"

"Well—not literally, I suppose," said Mrs. Ingram rather doubtfully. "No, of course not. But women who want to get married, and can't, often turn very queer as they grow older."

Monica felt little beads of cold sweat pricking at the roots of her hair.

"Frederica says she doesn't like men."

"Of course," Mrs. Ingram replied impatiently. "They always say that. She'd sing a very different tune if any man ever looked her way."

Monica knew how true it was.

"It seems a pity they can't do something—take up a hobby, or anything."

"Neither of them is much good at anything, I shouldn't think," said Mrs. Ingram mercilessly. "Besides, darling, when all's said and done, there's only one job for any woman, whether she's stupid or clever, and that is to be a good wife to some man and the mother of his children."

"And there aren't enough men to go round!" exclaimed Monica bitterly.

"*Don't*——" broke involuntarily from her mother.

They went into the house, avoiding one another's eyes. It was very seldom indeed that they came as near as they had come then to a direct mention of the subject that was always present in the minds of both.

That afternoon, Carol Anderson called to see Monica. With an air of charming concern he told her that she looked tired.

"You aren't going to be ill, are you? There's such a lot of influenza about."

"I know. We went to ask after Lady Marlowe this morning. But I don't see why I should get it at all. I haven't been anywhere near it."

"I don't know what I should do," said Carol Anderson very seriously, "if anything was the matter with you, and I couldn't see you. It makes such a tremendous difference to me, having you to talk to. Writing could never be the same thing."

"I like to think I'm a help to you," said Monica, quite truly.

"If ever you disappointed me in any way, Monica, you'd be

156

doing something worse than you probably have any idea of. I take things much, much more seriously than the average man does. I think you know that. Very probably I shouldn't reproach you at all. I might say nothing to you whatever. But the effect would be there—beyond your control or mine."

For the first time, she felt a little impatient with Carol's solemnities.

"I hope neither of us will disappoint the other," she returned tritely.

No one could be quicker than Carol Anderson to detect the finest shade of difference in a meaning, in an intonation even. He looked at her quickly.

"Do you say that because you *are* disappointed in me? If so, I'd much rather you told me so. Don't be afraid of hurting me. I can stand being hurt. I've borne a great deal already—and without letting anyone know it—and I can bear more, if necessary."

He squared his shoulders in his favourite gesture.

"But it isn't necessary, Carol. Truly. Don't be silly," said Monica rather timidly. "Of course I'm not disappointed in you."

It did not even occur to her for a moment that she was, actually, speaking an untruth. Her only preoccupation was the ingrained one: not to run any risk of losing her hold, however tenuous, on the interest of an unmarried male.

"I'm glad," said Carol, apparently accepting her reassurance. And he added, smiling a little:

"I didn't exactly see how you *could* be disappointed in me, I must say, because I've never given my confidence to anybody as I have to you."

He continued to give her his confidence.

Monica's frail self-respect continued to derive sustenance from his continual demands upon her. She wanted the Marlowes to see Carol, with his evident liking for her, and dependence on her, but it was not easy to arrange.

Lady Marlowe took some little while to recover from her influenza, and before she was out of her room, Frederica was suddenly and violently attacked by the same germ.

157

"Serve her right," said Mrs. Ingram unsympathetically. "The idiot might just as well have left her mother to Rouse and the nurse. I'm sure she was no use whatever, and now look at all the extra trouble she's giving! I suppose Cecily will want to go and nurse Fricky, and then she'll get it, and the whole thing will go on and on like a merry-go-round."

"I should think that if Cecily tries to nurse Fricky, or go near her," said Monica, "Fricky will be perfectly frantic. You know the fuss she made before—wanting her out of the house, and all that."

"I've no patience with her. Still, better ring up to-night and find out how she is, and if we can do anything."

Monica rang up Cecily, and made all enquiries. Cecily, her voice expressionless, said that the hospital nurse was looking after Frederica, and that she was sleeping most of the time.

"Are you—do you—sit with her?" hazarded Monica.

"No."

That was all. Cecily offered no explanation. It was entirely characteristic of her life-long allegiance to her tyrant not even to comment upon a circumstance of which Monica knew the inner cause as well as she did herself.

She only added that Dr. Corderey was being very kind.

"He thinks we ought to go away for a change after all this."

"Abroad? That would be nice."

"Yes. Of course it all depends on mamma. She hasn't said anything about it yet."

Cecily sounded neither more nor less dreary than usual. Monica, hanging up the receiver, reflected that to go abroad with Lady Marlowe as one of two unmarriageable daughters would probably be worse than to remain at home as usual.

CHAPTER IV

Mr. INGRAM, who was not nervous where infection was concerned, was quite ready to let Monica go round to Belgrave Square whenever she liked.

The London routine of parties and visits had long ago been dropped. It was better, the Ingrams tacitly decided, that Monica should have her own friends, and her own occupations, rather than that she should strenuously fulfil the obligations of season after season amongst a crowd of younger girls.

She had friends—not very intimate ones, for most of her contemporaries had married, and Monica could not bear to see them too often—and she manufactured occupations. There were always small shopping errands to be done, the flowers to be arranged, occasional visits to picture galleries and Exhibitions, and Sunday afternoon concerts. At one time Monica had attended a series of Red Cross lectures, with a view to learning First Aid. The classes were attended entirely by women, and she found them very dull. As Mrs. Ingram said, they led to nothing.

It was really a relief to Monica to go and sit with Cecily in the dreary Belgrave Square drawing-room, or to walk round the Square garden with her.

They had known one another so long that they could be almost natural together, and it was easier still in the absence of Frederica's bitter, scornful tongue and perpetual air of tragedy.

"How is Fricky?" Monica enquired perfunctorily every afternoon, and even more perfunctorily: "How is Lady Marlowe?"

Lady Marlowe was taking her time. She liked the hospital nurse who was looking after her, and had turned the care of

Frederica over to the severe and elderly maid, Rouse. Cecily did not see her sister, and only paid her mother a short visit morning and evening.

She appeared to have nothing whatever to do, but she was not unhappy. It seemed to Monica, on the contrary, that Cecily was looking less miserable. Once or twice she made suggestions, such as she would not have ventured on in Frederica's presence, for a walk in Kensington Gardens, to watch the children playing there. Monica, obscurely moved, always avoided the sight of young children, and she was surprised that Cecily should care to go and look at them. But Cecily seemed happier than usual, watching the shouting, running, woolly-clad babies, and their smart, uniformed nurses.

On a mild afternoon in late autumn, they walked across the Park together, returning to Belgrave Square for tea.

The small, neat car of Dr. Corderey stood at the door.

"Shall I go?" suggested Monica.

"Oh no. He only stays a few minutes. He'll just come in and tell me everything's all right," said Cecily.

She stood by the table in the hall, listlessly opening a couple of circulars. There was a rapid tread on the stairs above, and Dr. Corderey came quickly down.

Although he had been moving so rapidly, he did not seem to be in a hurry, but stood and talked cheerfully, giving an excellent account of both patients.

"Your mother talks of Brighton on Saturday, and I think that would be a very good idea. I've persuaded her to take her maid with her, and leave Nurse Hopkins here for Miss Marlowe."

"Shall we join her later, then—my sister and I?"

"I think it would be a very good idea if your sister had a change—and you too."

Something in Dr. Corderey's tone struck Monica, and she looked at him. He was watching Cecily with the same air of close professional attention that she had observed once before.

"Are you particularly busy just now?" he suddenly enquired.

"Not at all," said Cecily, startled.

"Then may I have a word with you? About this change of air, and so on," he added, as if to reassure her.

"Won't you come up to the drawing-room? Will you—will you have some tea?" Cecily asked doubtfully.

Monica, too, would have felt doubtful at making such a suggestion, but Dr. Corderey was apparently not doubtful at all, and he accepted the offer briefly and matter-of-factly.

Cecily poured out tea with fumbling, ill-assured gestures, and the doctor handed tea-cakes and bread-and-butter. He talked quietly on indifferent subjects.

Monica began to feel that she liked him. Not quite—quite, of course, but he seemed nice, and very kind, and she had an idea, for which she could have offered no reasonable grounds, that he must be clever.

He began to speak, about books, and she found, to her great surprise, that he had been lending books to Cecily. Poetry. He asked Cecily's opinion, and she gave it. Monica realized that it was almost the only time she had ever heard Cecily assert an independent view of her own. Perhaps she had held independent views in her own mind—but she had not hitherto dared to put them into words.

"Do you read a great deal, Miss Marlowe?"

"Not a great deal—I garden—at home," said Cecily.

"At home—that's in Yorkshire. Are you there most of the time?"

"Yes. We like it better than London," said Cecily quickly.

"You and your sister. Tell me, have you ever been separated from your sister?"

"No," said Cecily, colouring deeply, her hands moving uneasily.

"You were never sent to school, either of you?"

"Oh no."

"Well," said the doctor abruptly, "it's a great pity."

Monica felt as though he had suddenly caused a bomb to explode at their feet.

In the mysterious world of morbid reticences, artificial loyalties, and tortured nervous sensibilities that made up life for Frederica and Cecily Marlowe it was never admitted that they could ever have been better apart.

"You see," said the doctor, and he now addressed himself to Monica rather than to Cecily, "the very best thing for Miss Marlowe, when she's a little stronger, would be to get right away. She's not in a satisfactory condition, as regards her nerves. In fact, I should very much like to persuade Lady Marlowe to let her take a—kind of rest-cure, in the country, at a place I know well. But Miss Marlowe is a difficult patient, and she's got *you*——" he indicated Cecily, "very much on her mind. So what I want to be able to tell her, is that you've arranged a pleasant change of some kind for yourself. Then perhaps her mind would be at rest, and we could get her to pay rather more attention to what we want for her."

"Is Frederica very ill?" said Monica, puzzled. "Is there much wrong with her?"

"She's getting over her influenza very nicely."

"But is there something else?"

The nervous movements of Cecily's hands had ceased, and at Monica's question she lifted her head, and met Dr. Corderey's gaze in full.

"I think, please, I'd like to know exactly what you mean."

"*Really?*" he asked, with a peculiar emphasis.

Monica did not understand what he meant, but she saw that Cecily did.

"Yes, really."

Dr. Corderey, never taking his eyes off Cecily's face, began to speak very slowly and evenly.

"Your sister is not very far off a bad nervous breakdown. We can stave it off, of course—this illness has probably done

162

so. But sooner or later, it'll happen, if she goes on living this kind of life. She's a naturally nervous, highly-strung subject, and from what I can tell she has had no emotional outlet for years—if ever."

"Except—me," said Cecily, very low.

"Except you. I'm glad you spoke of that because, you see," said Dr. Corderey, very cheerfully, "I want to save you, if I possibly can, from her."

"But you can't," said Cecily. "No one can." She began to cry.

"Cecily! Don't!" Monica cried anxiously. She only half understood what was happening.

"Don't stop her. Let her cry, if she wants to," said the doctor.

He got up and stood beside Cecily's shaking figure, huddled on the sofa, and took her wrist professionally between his finger and thumb.

"Let her have it out. It won't do her any harm. Do you know anything about sick nursing?"

"No," said Monica.

"I suppose you were never sent to school either, and you live at home, and have nothing to do—except what you make for yourself—and if you were forced to earn your own living to-morrow, you'd have to starve."

Monica, for an instant, felt offended, because she knew that her mother would think she ought to be offended. But he had spoken with so much sincerity that she could not pretend to disagree.

"It's quite true."

"It's true of hundreds of others too. Thousands, I expect. Women come to me with every sort and kind of trouble—insomnia, and indigestion, and other things—and I do what I can for them. But what's really the matter with them is that they're unhappy. It's mind, not body."

He released Cecily's hand, and pushed her gently back amongst the sofa-cushions.

"It's all right. Keep still for a few minutes. Tell me, Miss

163

Ingram, could you get away from London for a week or two?"

"I think so." Monica considered. "Go somewhere with Cecily, you mean?"

"Yes. Abroad if you like. Switzerland—any bracing places."

Monica felt no certainty of obtaining her mother's permission. As long as she remained unmarried she would be regarded by her parents as requiring supervision.

Cecily raised her disfigured face.

"We shouldn't be allowed to go abroad, I don't think," she said simply. "Not by ourselves."

"Do you never do anything that you're not allowed to do?" the doctor enquired.

"Not often," Cecily admitted, smiling faintly.

"Then it's a very great pity. I'd like to see you rebel against everything that you've ever been told and defy everyone and—and generally throw your cap over the windmill. Perhaps," suggested Dr. Corderey, "some day, I shall?"

Cecily shook her head.

The tear-stains on her face, curiously enough, made her look very young.

"Well, think about what I've said. I want you to go right away somewhere with a friend of your own, and have a thorough change."

"But Frederica——"

"I'll look after Frederica," said the doctor curtly, and seeming unaware that he was referring to the daughter of the house by her Christian name.

Almost immediately afterwards he went away.

"Would you really like to go away somewhere, Cecily? You've never been anywhere without Frederica, have you?"

"Never."

"I don't suppose she'd—like it, would she? I mean, she's rather jealous of your having anything to do with anybody else."

"Yes, I know."

It was evident that Cecily, as usual, was either unwilling, or unable, to commit herself.

Monica did not repeat anything that Dr. Corderey had said at home. She thought about it very often, and could not decide whether she agreed with Dr. Corderey, or distrusted him as her mother would have done. The idea sometimes crossed her mind that, if he had been a gentleman—she meant, someone belonging to her own world—she might have fallen in love with him. Some thought of the kind went through Monica's mind with reference to every unmarried man that she ever met, but she was scarcely aware of it, any more than she realized that whenever she bowed to the new moon, or ate the first strawberry of the year, the automatic formula that sprang to her lips was always: *"I wish to be engaged to be married."*

No suggestion came from Belgrave Square, and Monica hoped that none might. She did not in the least want to go away into the country with Cecily Marlowe, and she was certain that they would not be allowed to go abroad together. And even if they were, nothing would happen. Cecily was not the kind of person with whom anything ever did happen.

Even now, Monica instinctively disassociated herself from Frederica and Cecily, when she thought in terms of romantic adventure. She could not believe herself to be as unattractive, as lacking in all magnetism, as she felt them to be.

Only sometimes, lying awake at night, she realized with terror that the years were slipping by—and no one had wanted to marry her.

"What ridiculous nonsense!" said Mrs. Ingram.

"What, mother?"

Even Vernon Ingram looked at his wife across the breakfast table and enquired also: "What is it, dear?"

"Poor Theodora Marlowe—as if she hadn't had worry enough over those two tiresome girls! Though it's absurd to call them girls, I'm sure. She writes very amusingly—she's always amusing—but I can see she's vexed. Dr. Corderey, if you please, has taken upon himself to give her some extremely unnecessary, and rather impertinent, advice about Frederica and Cecily."

"What advice?" asked Monica, remembering the little scene that she had witnessed in the Belgrave Square drawing-room.

"Some modern nonsense, darling, about nerves and fancies. He thinks it's very bad for them to be together all the time, as of course they are, and he wants Frederica to do a rest-cure, or something of the kind. He told Lady Marlowe that Cecily ought to be given a chance to get right away, on her own, and find something to do. As if there was anything she *could* do!"

"But, mother—they are rather odd, both of them. Perhaps it really would be a good thing——?"

"The only thing that would do either of them any good would be to find a husband," said Mrs. Ingram calmly. "And I don't suppose there's the slightest chance of that. I wish old Dr. Bruce had attended them himself, instead of sending this absurd young man. There's one thing, he'll never get sent for again. Lady Marlowe is very much annoyed with him."

Monica could quite well believe it. She knew that Lady Marlowe was quite unaccustomed to criticism, and would resent it the more where her two unsatisfactory daughters were concerned.

She sent for Frederica and the hospital nurse to join her at Brighton, and ordered Cecily to return to Yorkshire.

"I can't have two unmarried daughters trailing about the Metropole Hotel after me," wrote Lady Marlowe, very decidedly, to Mrs. Ingram. "Why on earth couldn't even *one* of them have been a son?"

Why indeed, wondered Monica. People were proud of their sons, whether they married or not. No woman minded being seen about with a son—far from it. But daughters, she

166

knew, were a very different thing. Even one daughter was bad enough.

After Frederica and the nurse had gone to Brighton and Cecily had returned, unprotesting, to Yorkshire and the company of the permanently resident ex-governess there, Monica's daily life went on, undisturbed by any event of importance.

CHAPTER V

THEN, quite suddenly, there was an accident.

Monica's father, returning from the Club one evening as usual, was knocked down by a taxi in the street.

Vernon Ingram was brought home unconscious.

He lay in a darkened room, knowing nothing, and in a moment, as it seemed, the lives of all of them had altered.

Nothing was of importance now excepting the life that was threatened. Examination revealed internal injuries, and it was feared that they were grave.

Monica sat downstairs, and answered the telephone, and wrote notes, and occasionally saw some of the people who came daily to enquire.

Most of them were relations, elderly and depressing.

On the third afternoon Monica was by herself, oppressed and unhappy, and vaguely wishing that Carol Anderson would come.

A card was brought in to her and her spirit knew a moment's lightening. She took it up eagerly and read the name of Mr. Pelham.

"Mr. Pelham asked if you would see him for a few minutes, Miss."

"Very well. Show him up."

She was disappointed, but it would be a relief to talk to anybody.

Mr. Pelham's gravity was habitual, and it was only slightly deepened as he came into the room and limply shook Monica's hand.

"How is he?"

"The same, thank you. He's conscious now—more or less.

He was concussed, you know, as well as being hurt in—other ways."

Monica had repeated these, and similar, phrases so often that she hardly felt as though she knew what she was saying.

"It must be a most anxious time for you. How is your mother?"

"She's wonderful," Monica repeated mechanically. "She's with him now. Of course there's a nurse as well."

"Of course."

"Won't you sit down? I dare say mother will be down in a few minutes. I asked them to let her know you were here."

"Thank you."

Mr. Pelham sat down, with his habitual gesture of carefully pulling up the knees of his trousers.

"What exactly happened? It was a cab, wasn't it?"

"As far as we know——" began Monica.

She recapitulated the story of the accident. She had been asked the same questions, and had given the same replies, many times in the past three days.

"I see," said Mr. Pelham at intervals, and "Really—yes—I suppose so," in a concerned voice.

His prawn-like eyes were fixed, inexpressively, upon Monica's face, and from time to time he nodded as if to show that he was paying attention to all she said.

Monica, as a matter of fact, had no doubts at all of his attention. She knew that Mr. Pelham had an extremely and unusually retentive memory. He often surprised her by reminding her of quite trivial conversations that they had exchanged in the course of the years that they had known one another.

"These cases of concussion are most curious. I remember a cousin of mine, once——"

Monica listened, rather wearily. Almost everyone had had some similar instance, a case of concussion, about which to tell her. Mr. Pelham's cousin had fallen on the back of his head, skating at Prince's. . . .

Monica, in her turn, said "Yes" and "I see."

In spite of herself, her thoughts wandered.

Carol had telephoned enquiries twice, and on the last occasion she had spoken to him, and said that she would like to see him. He had promised to come that afternoon, and she hoped he would not arrive until Mr. Pelham had gone.

Mr. Pelham was in no haste to go. He was always apt to pay lengthy visits, and Monica had rashly admitted that she had nothing to do.

At last she felt obliged to offer him tea.

"Thank you—that's very kind of you. But I don't wish—I know you must have letters to write—or perhaps you're wanted upstairs?"

"No," said Monica. "He doesn't really want anyone, you know. He's under morphia most of the time. To-morrow the doctors are hoping to make a more thorough examination, to see what can be done."

"Ah yes. I see."

Mr. Pelham looked graver than ever. He did not attempt to go away.

Just as tea was brought in, Carol Anderson came. His warm, long pressure of the hand brought a faint sensation of comfort to Monica. His questions were almost the same as those of Mr. Pelham, but he put them with an effect of urgency, and there was nothing inexpressive in the gaze that he fastened upon Monica whilst she replied.

"I'm so sorry for you," he said gently. "It must be dreadful for you. Is there anything in the world that I can do to help you, Monica?"

There was nothing, and she said so. But his earnestness had comforted her. She felt that he cared deeply about what had happened, for her sake.

Mrs. Ingram came down to tea looking pale and exhausted. The same things were said, again and again, by them all. She repeated that there was little change in her husband's condition. The doctors were hoping to make a further examination next day.

170

"At least he's not in pain. That's my great comfort," she kept on saying.

"It's wonderful what *can* be done nowadays," Mr. Pelham reiterated with equal persistence.

Carol Anderson carried a cup of tea to Monica, and made her the object of his care, telling her gently in an undertone that she *must* eat something. His solicitiude touched her, and sent a thrill of happiness through her.

"You won't go just yet, will you?" she murmured, looking up at him.

She meant that she hoped he would outstay Mr. Pelham.

"Of course I'll stay, if you'll let me. I want to," he replied gently.

Monica was almost ashamed of the quick response that his words, and still more his look, woke in her. She wanted to think only of her father, not of herself, nor even of Carol Anderson in relation to herself. But as long as he remained beside her, saying very little but every now and then looking at her anxiously and affectionately, she knew that she was happy.

She hoped urgently that when her mother made a move to return upstairs again, Mr. Pelham would go.

Mrs. Ingram however sat on in the corner of the sofa, finding relaxation in the change of atmosphere.

At last Mr. Pelham said, "Well——" in a tentative fashion, and sketched a movement towards rising.

"I suppose I ought to be going. Please let me know if there's any—any change. Perhaps you'll allow me to come round to-morrow?"

Mrs. Ingram assented. Monica was only intent on seeing him go away.

"Good-bye. I do so hope that you'll have better news in the morning."

He had shaken hands—the moist limpness of his touch was always faintly distasteful to Monica—and her mother had signed to her to ring the bell, in order that the servants might know he was going.

171

"Good-bye—so kind of you to come."

Mrs. Ingram did not sit down again when Mr. Pelham had made his exit. She remained as though uncertain, standing in the middle of the room.

"Shall I take your place for a little while, and send nurse downstairs?" Monica suggested.

She did not make the suggestion sincerely, for Mrs. Ingram was very jealous of her own supremacy in the sick-room, and did not allow Monica to share it.

"No, darling, no. Thank you. Dear father likes me to be there, when he comes to himself a little. I think I must go back now."

She rustled slowly from the room.

For the first time in her life, perhaps, thought Monica, her mother seemed really unaware that she was leaving her alone in the room with an eligible young man.

"She's wonderful, isn't she," said Carol respectfully.

He pushed an arm-chair closer to the fire.

"Sit down and rest, Monica. May I stay a few minutes longer?"

"Oh, please do."

Monica's habitual self-consciousness was loosened, in the relaxed mood following on the shock of the accident, and she was neither startled nor alarmed when Carol Anderson drew a small chair very close to hers, and took her hand in his.

"I'm so awfully sorry for you, dear. I do so understand what you're going through. Quite apart from the fact that I've had a good deal of personal experience of illness and anxiety, I seem to know by intuition *exactly* what my friends feel, when they're in great trouble. It's a most extraordinary thing, Monica, but it's as if I could see inside their minds. For instance, I know exactly what your mother is experiencing, when she sits upstairs, watching him. I know what you're feeling now, perhaps almost better than you know yourself."

Monica was accustomed to Carol's strange conviction of his own infallibility, and still stranger candour in proclaiming it. She was, in fact, deriving a warm and blessed sense of

172

comfort from the close hold of his hand over hers, and listening very little to what he was saying.

Presently she understood that he was telling her about the illness and death of a friend at Cambridge. It was Carol, it seemed, who had nursed him, remained with him to the end, and been the only person responsible for the trying formalities connected with sending the young man's body to his home in the North of Ireland.

"I was only twenty-one, actually, but I seemed able to do it all somehow. It had to be done, and I was the only person available, and so I simply went through with it. After it was all over I thought: Well, if I can do a thing like that I can do *anything*. It showed me my own strength, I suppose. That was lucky, perhaps, if I'd only known it."

In the silence that followed, Monica seemed to hear Viola Lester's name as clearly as though it had been spoken.

She sighed, moved restlessly, and broke the spell.

"I'm going to leave you, now. Are you a little bit less unhappy than when I came?"

"Yes," she replied with truth.

"I can nearly always do that," said Carol very gently, as he rose to his feet. "It's something—I don't exactly know what—that goes out from me to the other person. I'm glad I've helped you, Monica."

A week from the day of his accident, Vernon Ingram died, scarcely recovering consciousness.

Examination had revealed the hopelessness of the case, and Mrs. Ingram had been prepared by the doctors for her husband's death. She had, at first, seemed very brave.

"If only he doesn't have to suffer, I can bear anything," she kept on repeating.

Vernon Ingram did not have to suffer. The internal injuries that he had sustained were of such a nature as to make the case hopeless, and there was no attempt to do more than save him, as far as possible, from pain. The doctors used morphia freely.

Monica went in to see him, and he did not know her.

173

"Perhaps to-morrow," said the nurse compassionately.

She was an elderly woman, and—taking her cue from Mrs. Ingram—evidently regarded Monica as an utterly inexperienced girl, to be kept in ignorance as long as possible of the shadow that was hourly drawing closer to the house.

Monica, in fact, felt unable to realize the approach of death. Ever since she could remember, her father and mother had been there—part of the fabric of existence. She could not imagine one of them without the other.

She went up to bed on the night of her father's death, in obedience to her mother's injunction, believing still in a childish way that in the morning, somehow, there would be hope.

Even the familiar bedroom, that had been hers ever since she had outgrown a nurse and a night-nursery, offered a silent testimony that violent and radical change held no place in her life. Pink silk, brass, and white-painted furniture still predominated. The wall-paper, originally a pattern of pink roses and silver trellis-work, had been replaced by a very modern one—birds, of an unspecified variety, hovering amongst branches from which hung clusters of a fruit that Monica always supposed, rather vaguely, to be some kind of pomegranate. The colour of these "toned in" with the pink curtains and the china on the wash-stand.

The embossed silver set of brushes and boxes, with the heads of angels on the backs, still lay on the dressing-table.

The picture of Napoleon, that had once testified to Monica's first act of independence, had long ago disappeared. It had been replaced, in fact, several times, as different cults had taken Monica's fancy. For a long while, now, she had had hanging against the wall a reproduction of *The Laughing Cavalier*. There was a faint resemblance to Carol Anderson in the set of the head.

The thought of Carol comforted her, for he had shown her great affection and sympathy, and had been to the house continually.

Perhaps, she thought dimly, her trouble would bring him

174

closer to her. She did not expect to take Viola Lester's place in Carol's imagination, for it was evident enough that only the unattainable could ever really satisfy his yearnings for romance, but she would have been more than content to accept anything that he cared to offer her.

Nobody wanted to marry her, and Monica's deepening terror and dismay told her that, if she could not marry—and the chances of it were lessening year by year—there was very little left for her in life.

She pushed the thought away from her with all her might, and went to bed.

A familiar dream visited her.

She was in the dining-room downstairs, and reading a copy of *The Morning Post*, and saw in it the announcement of her own forthcoming marriage. As usual, in the dream, the name of the man she was to marry was a blur. She was conscious of dismay and disappointment because she could not remember having received a proposal, nor an engagement ring, but at the same time she felt glad, because she was going to be married at last and her parents would be so pleased. She could hear her father coming downstairs, step by step, and turned to the door, waiting to see him come in and to greet him with her joyful tidings. The steps grew louder and louder, and it seemed as if the house shook with them. . . .

"Miss Ingram—Miss Ingram. . . ."

Someone was knocking at her door.

"What is it?" Monica, confused and startled, sprang out of bed, switching on the light as she did so.

"Better come down. Quickly, my dear—he's going fast." The feet of the nurse retreated swiftly down the stairs again.

Monica threw on her dressing-gown and followed her. The lights on both landings were burning, and the door of her father's room stood open.

Her mother was kneeling by the bed and the nurse stood beside her. The bandaged figure on the pillows lay quite still, but the sound of heavy breathing was loud in the dim room. Monica, trembling violently, went close to the head of the bed.

175

"Can't anything be done?" she whispered, agonizedly.

The nurse shook her head.

"He can't feel anything. He's not conscious," she said.

The tiny clock on the mantelpiece chimed two. Another sound mingled with it and then ceased.

For a moment Monica did not understand what had happened.

Then she saw her mother's dark head—still with its elaborate coils and curls dressed as she wore it every day—sink to the pillow.

"She's fainted—the very best thing she could have done," said the nurse, in hushed tones. "I should like to get her on to her bed before she comes round."

Between them, they took Mrs. Ingram into her room, and Monica rang the upstairs bell for Parsons.

"Had we better send for the doctor?" she whispered piteously.

"No, no. He can't do anything for——" the nurse signed with her head towards the other room. "Your mother's worn out, that's what it is, with the strain. She'll be round in a few minutes. I want a hot drink for her, and for you too, Miss Ingram."

Parsons came down, and although she at once began to cry, she was practical and helpful, knew where to find a small flask of brandy, and heated some milk on the spirit-lamp.

The nurse occupied herself with Mrs. Ingram, who came to, shivering and moaning, and presently broke into hysterical screaming and sobbing.

It took the nurse a long while to quiet her, and to persuade her to let herself be undressed and put into bed.

"Stay with her, Miss Ingram. I must go back," said the nurse.

"Shall I come and lie down beside you, mother?"

"If you like. It's dreadful—dreadful! I can't believe it. Oh, Monica—Monica——!"

She was screaming again, stifling the sound in the pillow, throwing herself about, and clutching wildly at Monica.

176

The hours passed, hideous as a nightmare. Mrs. Ingram would not rest for an instant, nor allow Monica to do so. When she was not crying and exclaiming hysterically, she poured out a torrent of words, partly reminiscences of her married life, and partly a series of assertions to the effect that she could not live, Monica must not expect her to survive the agony of her loss.

The self-control that she had manifested throughout the past week had deserted her completely.

Monica tried hard to cry, and could not. She was principally conscious of feeling sick, and continued to shiver spasmodically.

Time passed with incredible slowness. Monica thought that it must be nearly six o'clock and that the servants would soon be stirring, and then turned on the light to look at the clock, and saw that it was barely four. She wondered if the clock could have stopped, but the hands of her mother's watch pointed to the same hour.

Presently the nurse came in, asked if she could do anything, and said that she had sent Parsons back to bed and would get some sleep herself.

"You'll be having your tea brought in at eight," she said hopefully. "Try and get some sleep, won't you. Why not let me give you some aspirin, Mrs. Ingram?"

She fetched the aspirin, and Mrs. Ingram took it, protesting and sobbing all the time. The nurse soothed her, speaking with an assumption of professional authority that quieted Mrs. Ingram for a little while.

Afterwards, when the nurse had left them, she lay back in the bed, but continued to turn and twist restlessly, every now and then breaking into fresh sobs, and ceaselessly talking without pausing for any reply.

Two or three times between four o'clock and six Monica fell into an uneasy doze, but always to be roused by the sobbing, tossing woman at her side.

At last, as soon as she heard sounds of movement in the house, Monica got up and went to her own room.

She felt stiff and chilled, as though she had been up and dressed all night long.

As she dressed, she remembered with startled astonishment that she ought to put on a black dress. She could only find a black serge skirt and a grey satin blouse, with a black bow in the front of the square sailor collar. She found that she dreaded a return to her mother, but she was ashamed of the feeling, and went down at once. To her intense relief, Mrs. Ingram had fallen into a heavy sleep. She did not wake until the arrival of the doctor, summoned by telephone soon after eight o'clock.

CHAPTER VI

"You must be your mother's comfort now, Monica. You're all she has left."

Almost every relation and friend of the Ingrams said that to Monica.

They had attended Vernon Ingram's funeral, and had sent quantities of expensive wreaths and crosses and anchors made of flowers, and many of them had come back to the house afterwards and had gone, one by one, to sit for a few minutes with the widow, in her small boudoir on the second floor, while Monica remained, with the throng of black-clad relations, in the library downstairs.

The day after the funeral she and her mother went away, to rooms on the south coast.

It was early in the year, and bitterly cold. Cousin Blanche, who had suggested the place and had recommended the rooms, assured them that it would be much warmer than in London, and that it was quiet a place where they would see nobody, and could go for walks in the sun and breathe the sea air.

Monica, ever afterwards, remembered that fortnight as one of perpetual physical misery. It seemed to her that they spent all their time in trying to coax an unwilling fire to burn, and finding tepid water in their rooms at night. Twice they changed their lodgings, but nowhere could they find warmth. Parsons caught a heavy cold and was so miserable that Mrs. Ingram sent her back to London, but obstinately refused to return there herself. She said that she could not face the changed house.

Day after day, in the sitting-room where the window-frames rattled wildly under the onslaughts of a perpetual north-east wind, Monica and Mrs. Ingram sat, with black-edged notepaper and envelopes strewing the tables and chairs, and answered innumerable letters of condolence, continually interrupted by outbursts of tears from the widow.

There was a great similarity in all the letters that they had received. Monica felt that it could hardly be otherwise. Some of the writers made the mistake of referring to their own experience of loss and sorrow.

"Your feet are now treading the thorny path that mine trod nearly ten years ago. . . ."

"I think you know that I too have known what it is to lose all that I held most dear in life——"

Those letters Mrs. Ingram read with tightened lips and an air of unspoken resentment. She replied to them, however, as to all the others—long, long answers that covered several sheets of the black-bordered paper, and that were frequently blotted with tears, so that she had to write them, or part of them, over again.

Monica had letters of her own to answer, but the ones written by friends of her own generation were a good deal shorter than those of the older people.

"These young things who have never known sorrow," said Mrs. Ingram, with a kind of pitying superiority.

She saw most of Monica's replies; indeed it would have been almost impossible to avoid doing so in the vast accumulation of correspondence that seemed to flood their small sitting-room and single writing-table.

Monica did not resent it. She realized that these days of bereavement belonged exclusively to her mother, and that Mrs. Ingram took for granted her priority right in everything that concerned their loss.

The only letters that Monica was at pains to keep to herself were those that she received from Carol Anderson.

They were affectionately worded letters—he always began, Monica, my dear, and signed himself, Yours with love, Carol—but they often strayed into curiously unconvincing dissertations on books that he had been reading, plays that he had seen, or abstract questions that he declared himself to have analysed and answered. It was difficult to avoid the conclusion that he wrote hoping to impress his correspondent, and perhaps himself as well.

Monica felt a certain tenderness for Carol's vanity, when she permitted herself to recognize it. But if she sought, as she sometimes did, to idealize him, and endow him with qualities of strength, generosity, and sincerity, she was forced to admit that very often he chilled and disappointed her. It was evident that he would always take everything, and give very little in return. Monica continued to write to him, to think of him very often, and to wish despairingly that he would ask her to marry him.

The fortnight at the sea was the longest one that she had ever known. It seemed to become more impossible to achieve warmth every day. Mrs. Ingram was not accustomed to walking, and twenty minutes' slow progress along the sea front, battling against an icy wind, usually tired her out without improving the state of her circulation.

"Monica, I can't bear this wind any longer. It's not doing either of us any good—your face is blue, my child. Come indoors."

They went indoors, but except for the absence of the cutting wind it did not seem to be much warmer there. Draughts came in beneath doors, and through window-sashes, and the stairs and bedrooms achieved a degree of iciness that surpassed the sitting-room. It was only possible to keep warm in bed, each with a hot-water bottle, and all their heaviest coats spread over the blankets. Mrs. Ingram, however, was sleeping badly, and very often called Monica from the adjoining room in order that she might listen to an outpouring of despair, ending in a storm of sobs and tears.

By the time she had wept and talked herself into a state of exhaustion, and Monica could leave her, the hot-water bottle in the deserted bed had grown tepid and Monica, chilled and distressed, found it difficult to regain any degree of comfort.

It sometimes seemed to her as though, in the accumulated miseries of the moment, she almost lost her sense of personal sorrow at her father's death.

When she thought of him now, it was of him as he had seemed to her in her baby-days—a beneficent and omnipotent being of herculean proportions—rather than as the remote, conventionally affectionate father, of whose secret disappointment in his only child she had so long been bitterly aware.

Yet it seemed strange and sad, almost impossible indeed, to resume life in the familiar Eaton Square house without him. Mrs. Ingram continually repeated that nothing could ever, ever, be the same again.

It was a bitterly cold day when they travelled back to London, and Monica continually found herself looking forward eagerly to the warmth and comfort of their own house. The anticipation of physical well-being, actually, over-powered any sense of distress in returning to the sight of her father's vacant place.

At Victoria, a hat-box belonging to Mrs. Ingram was found to be missing.

"I'm certain it was put in—absolutely certain," declared the widow, over and over again. She hurried up and down the platform, her heavy furs held against her face to shield her from the raw, foggy air, compelling the porter to look repeatedly for the missing box in vans that he had already thoroughly searched.

Monica, cold and exasperated, clutching her mother's heavy green leather dressing-bag, followed her on heels that seemed suddenly to have grown too high, so that she leant forward at an insecure angle and tottered slightly in her thin patent-leather shoes.

"We must go to the Lost Luggage place," said Mrs. Ingram.

"Oh dear, this fog! Monica, can you remember seeing it actually *labelled*?"

"I think they labelled everything."

"Darling, what's the good of saying that? It isn't a question

182

of having labelled everything. I want to know if the *hat*-box was labelled."

"I'm afraid I don't remember."

"I'm perfectly certain it was. I saw to everything myself. I shall have to get accustomed to that now," said Mrs. Ingram bitterly.

Monica saw that her mother was preparing to cry. Intense nervous irritation clutched her, and she clenched her teeth in the effort to subdue it.

Mrs. Ingram fumbled amongst her belongings—muff, pocket, handbag, and jewel-case—for a handkerchief. She raised her veil and dabbed at her eyes.

"Here you are, lady," said the porter.

It took Mrs. Ingram more than twenty minutes to say all that she wished to say at the Lost Property Office, and to fill in the necessary form.

At last it was finished.

"Cab, lady?"

"There should be a car waiting."

"It's there, mother. I saw it," said Monica.

"Thank Heaven. I was beginning to feel that everything in the world was lost."

Mrs. Ingram cried all the way home.

She cried again, more violently, when the familiar library was reached and she had sunk into an arm-chair beside the fire.

Monica, kneeling in front of the welcome blaze and allowing the heat to penetrate through and through her, could feel nothing but intense physical relief.

In the train she had wondered wistfully if Carol Anderson would have thought of writing a letter to greet her on arrival. She did not think it likely. Affectionate and charming as he often showed himself towards her, he had but few moments of imaginative insight where anyone but himself was concerned.

The letters were brought in, and Monica looked through hers with a flicker of hope. Carol, however, had not written.

Monica thought: Men aren't like women. They never think of things like that. If *I* cared about anybody. . . .

There was a kind of stifled scream from Mrs. Ingram.

"Monica, Monica—oh, I can't bear it—they've sent—they've sent—*these*——"

Her pale ringed hands almost threw the papers at Monica, and then flew up to cover her convulsed face.

"How can I bear it—how *can* I go on living?" wailed Mrs. Ingram, rocking herself backwards and forwards.

Monica saw that in her lap were designs for a headstone. The firm had sent several drawings, as well as a covering letter and estimate of prices.

She looked at them with a queer feeling of unreality, envying her mother's violence of emotion.

"Give them to me," sobbed Mrs. Ingram.

"Won't you look at them to-morrow morning, mother? You must be very tired."

"What does it matter if I'm tired? What is there to save myself for now? My life is over—*over*," said Mrs. Ingram wildly.

For another hour she continued to weep and exclaim, alternately poring over the designs and pushing them violently away from her.

Then a message was brought in to say that there was a visitor downstairs.

Carol?

Monica's heart leapt.

But the card that was handed to Mrs. Ingram was that of old cousin Blanche.

At first, Mrs. Ingram declared that it was impossible to see her. It was too soon. The early days of bereavement should be sacred . . . then, with the revulsion of feeling characteristic of her unbalanced condition, she altered her mind.

"She's dear, dear father's relation—one of his family. I think he might have wished me to see her. Go down, Monica, and bring cousin Blanche in here to me. You must leave us alone, darling."

Ashamed of the unspeakable relief that rushed over her at the words, Monica left the room.

Cousin Blanche was grave, but not emotional. She kissed Monica, asked after her mother, and said: "You must be everything in the world to her now," and then went to Mrs. Ingram.

It was almost the first break in the continual *tête-à-tête* of the last three weeks, and Monica felt sick and weak with the relief of being alone and able to relax the ceaseless tension of day and night.

She went slowly up to her own room, took off her hat and sealskin jacket, and the tight, stiff patent-leather shoes, and dropped upon the bed in utter exhaustion.

Except for the fact that her nights, for the most part, were now her own again, it was the last hour of solitude that she was to know for many months.

Mrs. Ingram could not bear to be by herself.

She wanted to talk incessantly about herself, her loss, the devotion that had existed between herself and her husband, and her complete indifference to life and longing for death.

Everyone, Monica included, took it for granted that it was Monica's part to listen to her with unflagging sympathy, compassion, and reverence, and to remain close beside her always.

After their return to Eaton Square, life became easier, because friends and relations came to visit them, and after a little while it was possible to persuade Mrs. Ingram to return the visits. Once or twice she even proved willing to go and stay away for a few nights. Monica always went with her.

Time slipped away, slowly, monotonously, and irretrievably. One day Monica realized that her mother no longer said: "It was a month ago to-day . . . two months exactly since——"

Without knowing it, they had ceased to measure time from the day that Vernon Ingram had left them.

Routine established itself.

After the quarter-past-nine breakfast Mrs. Ingram interviewed the cook, and carried out all the duties of housekeeping, none of which she had ever delegated—for she continued to regard Monica as an irresponsible child. Afterwards she read the front page and Court Circular of the morning paper very carefully, commenting on the contents aloud to Monica, glanced at the headlines, said that the Suffragettes ought to be whipped at the cart's tail and that Ireland was more trouble than it was worth, and occasionally pursued some distinguished invalid, whose condition was reported, into the pages of Burke or Debrett.

At eleven o'clock Mrs. Ingram had a small tray brought to her with biscuits and a patent food, and Monica, unwillingly, had to drink a glass of milk. Her mother had decreed that milk was good for the complexion—although Monica's skin, actually, had long since lost all its glow and acquired a permanent clear pallor that made her look older than she was.

Soon afterwards they went out. There was always something to be done—flowers to be ordered from Sylvester's in Sloane Square, or wool from Head's in Sloane Street. Sometimes they went as far as Harrod's Stores, or, on fine mornings, for a turn in the Park.

Luncheon was at half-past one. Occasionally someone was asked to come, but usually they sat alone, waited on by the two men-servants, and with all the heavy silver, glass, and china put on the table just as had always been done.

After coffee in the library, Mrs. Ingram, by her doctor's orders, rested on the sofa. She was persuaded that she was a very bad sleeper, and would not admit that she ever dozed in the day-time, so that she liked Monica to remain in the library with her, in order that they might exchange occasional remarks.

Sometimes they went out driving in the afternoon, or to pay a call. Sometimes Mrs. Ingram wrote letters at the drawing-room writing-table, murmuring half to herself and half to Monica all the time.

"Army and Navy Stores—Army and Navy *Co-operative* Stores, I believe they call themselves—Victoria Street, S.W. Really, I wish I knew how the servants get through so much tea. I'm sure it's very bad for the maids, and I shall tell Mrs. Horben so. Army and Navy Co-operative . . . Dear me, that's the last envelope. . . . I hope I haven't run out of envelopes. Monica, just look in the bottom drawer of the lacquer cabinet, darling. . . . No, dear, mother said the *bottom* drawer. Don't you ever pay attention to what you're told? Well, then, look in the middle drawer. Or the top one, perhaps. I thought so. I knew there were some somewhere. But that's the last box. I'd better order some more."

"Shall I telephone?"

"No, darling, I'd better write. I never think the telephone is really safe; it's so easy for the shop to make a mistake, and then say they didn't hear what one said. No, I shall have to write. Messrs. Truslove & Hanson—Dear Sirs, Kindly send me—— How many do you think I'd better order, Monica?"

Mrs. Ingram frequently asked some such rhetorical question, but Monica knew very well that she did not really want her daughter's advice. Whatever reply she made her mother invariably received it with a shake of the head.

"Nonsense, darling. That wouldn't do. No, I'd better tell them. . . ."

Tea was brought to the drawing-room.

Quite often Carol Anderson came to see Monica, Mr. Pelham called and remained in solemn conversation for an hour, or old friends looked in and exchanged small items of news concerning acquaintances and relations.

These interruptions formed the most exciting events of Monica's life.

The evenings were usually trying. Monica could not fall back on her old resource of strumming on the piano, for if she did, Mrs. Ingram said that "music upset her" and began to cry.

She and her mother glanced desultorily through the new novels sent from Mudie's, or sometimes played patience

187

together. From half-past nine onwards, Mrs. Ingram glanced continually at the clock and wondered aloud if it was too early to go to bed.

At ten o'clock she went.

Monica had fallen into the habit of coming in to her to say good-night, and often remained talking of trivialities in Mrs. Ingram's room until midnight or later.

Then she would crawl upstairs, listless and yet exhausted, and fall asleep as soon as she got into bed.

Book Three

The Happy Ending

CHAPTER I

IT WAS Sunday afternoon, and Mr. Pelham, as usual, was paying a lengthy call on Mrs. and Miss Ingram.

His conversation, for once, was absorbing their entire attention, for he had just returned from a visit to Yorkshire and had astonishing news of the Marlowes.

"I was with the Duncombes, you understand, not staying with Lady Marlowe—but they're fairly near neighbours, and you know what an interest these good people who live in the country take in one another's business," said Mr. Pelham in a faintly admonitory tone that precluded any assumption that he might himself take any undue interest in his neighbour's affairs.

"Well, Cecily Marlowe has acquired a—a suitor."

"Is she engaged?" cried Monica. A frightful pang went through her.

"It must be somebody very unsuitable," said Mrs. Ingram shrewdly, "or her mother would have rushed them to the nearest church long ago."

"It *is* unsuitable," Mr. Pelham admitted, with a slight smile, "but not utterly impossible. I think you know the young man—a Dr. Corderey."

"Do you mean to say that he's had the impertinence to propose to Cecily Marlowe?"

"So I believe."

"Well," said Mrs. Ingram, recovering herself, "if she has any sense, she'd better take him. As I always say, any

189

husband is better than none at all, and those girls have been hanging about for years, and no one has ever looked at either of them. If I were her mother, I should let her marry him on the spot."

"Has she accepted him?" Monica asked.

"I believe so. There was a great deal of talk about it in the house-party at Cressfield—in fact, one or two of the younger people were laying bets about it—but no one knew anything definite. The—the principal source of information was the married daughter, Clemmie Godwin—she married Ingleton's eldest son about five years ago, if you remember—she's by way of being a friend of Frederica's."

"I suppose Frederica's tearing her hair. Really, I often wonder if she's quite all there," said Mrs. Ingram casually. "Do tell us some more, Mr. Pelham. It's really too amusing. What does poor dear Theodora think about it?"

"The general impression seems to be that she began by being perfectly furious, and then saw the funny side of it— she has such a wonderful sense of humour, of course—and now she's going about telling everyone that Cecily is quite old enough to know her own mind——"

"That's true, at all events!" ejaculated Mrs. Ingram.

"—And that if she likes to go and pour medicines out of bottles and help mix powders—she puts it in the most amusing way—why, nobody can very well forbid her to."

"Theodora is a very clever woman. She's thankful to get one of them off her hands at any price, and she knows how to make the best of a bad job. I must say, I should have thought Cecily would have written to you, Monica."

"So should I," said Monica coldly.

She was bewildered, bitterly jealous, and rather angry.

"Do you know how it happened?" she enquired of Mr. Pelham, who sat turning his head from one to the other of his listeners, his face immobile as ever, but a certain triumphant glistening in his prominent eyes, betokening satisfaction with himself and the sensation that he was creating.

"That's another very queer thing. I believe they met in London—he attended the house professionally——"

"Good Heavens, it was I who sent him!" cried Mrs. Ingram, with more animation in her voice and manner than had been there for many weeks.

"Not really?"

"Practically. He's partner to our own doctor, and went instead of him when they all had influenza."

"He went to some purpose," Mr. Pelham observed, with portentous humour.

"I should think so indeed! But do go on."

Mr. Pelham went on.

"I suppose that he was—attracted—then. He apparently made the most desperate efforts to get Cecily sent abroad or somewhere. Saying, you see, that it would be good for her health. Well, of course, she always has looked most terribly delicate—they both have, for that matter—but, as Lady Marlowe said, there's never been anything the matter with her all these years, so why should she suddenly have to go abroad? Especially as he was insistent about her going alone, without Frederica."

"He said once, in front of me, that they ought to be separated," put in Monica suddenly. "That it would be the best thing for them."

"Darling, I suppose Dr. Corderey doesn't know better than God Almighty," said her mother humorously. "*He* gave Cecily a sister, and as long as two sisters remain unmarried it seems only natural that they should be together, under the same roof. Blood is thicker than water, after all."

"I know, but——"

Mrs. Ingram made a quick gesture, silencing her. Monica's opinion was of no value, it was not respectful to argue with one's mother, and in any case she wanted to hear what more Mr. Pelham had to say.

"Most strangely," said Mr. Pelham impressively, "*most* strangely, it seems that Cecily and this fellow entered into a correspondence. He lent her books, or something, and I

191

suppose that led to their being sent back, and acknowledged, and so on. Not that I mean to say that there was anything in the least odd about that, if it had been someone in our own world, but really, as it was——"

"Did Fricky aid and abet her?"

"I'm certain Fricky didn't know anything about it," asserted Monica, at the risk of being told, in one of Mrs. Ingram's favourite phrases, not to lay down the law. She was remembering the passionate urgency with which Frederica had invariably sought to stand between her sister and experience in almost any shape.

Mr. Pelham nodded in assent.

"You're quite right, Miss Ingram. Absolutely right. Frederica was told nothing whatever about it, I believe. But as a matter of fact, she's acute, as you probably know, and she apparently guessed there was something up, so to speak, and moved heaven and earth to find out from Cecily what it was."

Monica shuddered slightly. Momentarily, she had an imaginative glimpse of that inquisition. . . .

"In fact it was the incessant friction between the two that led to the whole thing coming out."

"And then he proposed?" Mrs. Ingram suggested.

"He came straight up to Yorkshire. Unfortunately, nobody seems to know exactly what happened next. Clemmie Godwin was in Paris just then. Nothing has been given out, formally, but there's a general idea that something will be, quite soon."

"Certainly there's nothing to wait for. Very much the contrary. I dare say it's a very good thing, after all. He can't be marrying her for money, because every penny of it belongs to Theodora, and she needn't leave any of it to the girls unless she wants to, I believe. But I suppose she'll give Cecily an allowance."

"The rumour is," Mr. Pelham observed in surprised tones, "that the young man is quite well off himself. Private means, I suppose."

192

"All the better. Are they going to get married immediately, or announce the engagement, or what?"

"I don't quite know," repeated Mr. Pelham helplessly. "Nobody knows. But if it's true they're engaged, it's bound to be announced soon."

"I must say, I never expected either of those girls to get a husband. I don't mean to say a word against them—they're not bad-looking, or at least they weren't before they grew— how can I put it politely?—shall we call it, rather long in the tooth? But they've always been thoroughly odd, and unlike anybody else. I might have guessed that if either of them ever did marry, it would be certain to be the family grocer or somebody of that kind."

Mr. Pelham laughed politely.

"Hardly so bad as that, perhaps. But I really must be going. I've paid you a regular visitation, I'm afraid."

"You've been *most* interesting," Mrs. Ingram declared emphatically. "Do let us know if you hear anything more— though I feel sure Monica will get a letter. They were all three practically brought up together."

"Oh, of course you'll hear. That is, if there really is anything to hear. But I feel sure there's something in it personally. Well—I really must——"

Mr. Pelham shook hands, turned in the doorway to bow slightly once more, and took his departure.

"What a gossiping old woman he is," said Mrs. Ingram ungratefully. "Ring the bell, Monica."

"I have rung it."

For the remainder of the evening Mrs. Ingram seemed cheerful and interested, returning continually to the topic of Cecily Marlowe.

"Of course, it's a very bad match," she repeated several times, with unconscious satisfaction. And once she added: "I couldn't bear *you* to do anything like that, my darling."

Monica wondered bitterly whether her mother still really entertained any serious hope or expectation of seeing her married to anybody at all.

For her own part, she felt that there was little but despair in her heart.

The next morning she received a letter from Cecily. It merely said, in stilted and childish phraseology, that she was engaged to John Corderey, whom Monica would remember, and that they hoped to be married very soon but it wasn't quite settled when. Cecily hoped that Monica would come to her wedding. Not a word about Frederica.

There was a formal announcement of the engagement in *The Morning Post*.

"I'm glad she's had the decency to write," said Mrs. Ingram, rather indignantly; "but do you mean to say she hasn't asked you to be her bridesmaid?"

"I'm very glad she hasn't. I'm getting past the age for that kind of thing."

"Don't talk nonsense," said Mrs. Ingram curtly.

"I think Cecily might have told me rather more about it. She doesn't say anything at all except the bare fact."

"I suppose you'll be seeing her directly. She'll want to do her shopping here, even if the actual wedding is to be in Yorkshire. Doesn't she say anything about coming to London?"

"Nothing at all."

"How like a Marlowe to make unnecessary mysteries! Well, I suppose I must write to her mother, and try not to say 'Better late than never.' I wonder how Frederica is taking it."

Monica also wondered.

She wrote reproachfully to Cecily.

"I do think you might have told me some of the really *interesting* things about your engagement. After all the ages we've known each other, and talked about getting married! And you don't say a word about Fricky. I suppose that means she's been making the most terrible fuss about it all. I do hope you'll be happy, Cecily, and that he's very, very nice. I expect he is."

Monica felt that in writing thus to Cecily she was reverting to the outlook and the phraseology of their schoolroom days. She could neither help it nor understand why it should be so.

She was acutely miserable at the thought that Cecily was going to be married and that she herself was not. It added to her misery that she was ashamed of it, and despised and reproached herself for her unworthy jealousy. But nothing that she could do made it any less.

It surprised her vaguely that her mother, beyond saying once or twice that such a marriage as Cecily was making would have been out of the question for Monica, showed no signs of any similar distress.

A few days later, she understood.

Mrs. Ingram, in an access of midnight misery, such as she still occasionally indulged herself with, roamed up to Monica's bedroom, woke her by flashing on the light, and—after saying: "Don't wake up, darling; go to sleep again, it's nothing"—sat down on the foot of her bed.

She said that Monica was her only child—all that she had left in the world. Sometimes she thought that Monica might want to leave her, and she couldn't bear it.

"Not that I'd ever grudge you your happiness, my precious one, but just for a few years more—I don't suppose it'll be for very long."

Monica, sick with pity, understood.

Her mother wanted to save her face.

She wanted both of them to be able to say that Monica had deliberately chosen not to marry, so that she might devote herself to her mother.

"Mother!"

"What, dear?"

"Cecily's engagement is broken off again!"

Mrs. Ingram almost snatched the newspaper out of Monica's hands.

"Good Heavens! I always *said* the Marlowes were as mad as hatters. It was quite extraordinary enough to get engaged to her doctor without going and breaking it off, surely?"

"Do you suppose that Lady Marlowe——?"

"No, I don't," declared Mrs. Ingram energetically. "I'm sure she realized perfectly well that *any* marriage would be better than none, at this time of day. Besides, she's not at all the kind of person to change her mind—you know that as well as I do. If she once agreed to the marriage, which she did, the very last thing she'd want would be to let Cecily make a public fool of herself by breaking it all off again."

"Then," said Monica, "it's Fricky's doing."

"Could even Cecily be so idiotic as to let her elder sister prevent her from getting married? Besides, why should Frederica do a thing like that?"

"I don't know. Jealousy, perhaps. She never has wanted Cecily to have a life of her own. And if she made enough fuss about it, and said how dreadful it would be for her to be left alone, I think Cecily would give in."

"Then all I can say is, that if Cecily is as weak-minded as all that, she deserves all she'll get," said Mrs. Ingram.

Monica did not feel that her mother's arbitrary condemnation, justified though it might be, wholly covered the case.

She herself was perplexed and uneasy, and faintly ashamed of the definite relief that it occasioned her to know that Cecily, after all, was not going to be married. She neither wrote to Cecily nor received any letter from her, but a few weeks later Lady Marlowe suddenly appeared in London and came to see Mrs. Ingram. She spent a short quarter of an hour on conventional condolences, allowed Mrs. Ingram to talk about herself and her sorrow for ten minutes, and then, true to her reputation, began to be amusing.

"My dear, be thankful that your girl doesn't play you the tricks that mine play me. (Monica, I've always told Fricky and Cecily that you're worth both of them put together.) Imagine, if you can, my feelings at the way Cecily's made a laughing-stock of herself and me!"

"Oh, but of course not," Mrs. Ingram protested politely. "It's really such a mercy to have discovered that it wouldn't do, *before* the wedding-day instead of *after*."

She said it without much conviction, and Lady Marlowe laughed frankly.

"Nonsense, my dear. It's too sweet of you to put it like that, but you know my brutal frankness, and as I said to Cecily, when it turned out that the Corderey person had actually proposed—which I believe he did by letter—if you were eighteen, I said, and in your first season, it would be another thing altogether. One would simply tell one's nearest male relation to send him off with a flea in his ear. But when you'll never see thirty again, and there's never been so much as a nibble, from *anybody*, by far the best thing you can do is to accept him, and marry him as quickly as you decently can before he changes his mind."

"Did Cecily—care for him?" asked Monica.

"Oh yes, I think she thought herself very much in love," said Lady Marlowe, looking amused. "He was quite present-able, too—much better manners than one has oneself—that kind of person always has, I believe. But of course, you know him."

"I've always felt so guilty," Mrs. Ingram declared, "at having been responsible, in the first place, for his ever coming to you."

"But, my dear Imogen, not at all. Who, in Heaven's name, could have foreseen what happened? In fact, it couldn't have happened with anyone's daughter except mine. I'm sure I often wonder what sins in my past incarnations I must be expiating to have had only daughters—and *such* daughters!"

"You're always so amusing, Theodora, but it really is too bad of you to talk like that. Poor Cecily!"

"My dear, I think it's poor me. First of all I can't get either of them engaged to anyone, either for love or money, then Cecily says she wants to marry the doctor, then Frederica takes to her bed and has hysterics, and finally Cecily says she doesn't want to get married after all and breaks the whole thing off again."

"Then it was Frederica," said Monica, half under her breath.

Lady Marlowe heard, and gave her a shrewd look.

"You guessed, did you? How dreadfully poor Fricky does give herself away, doesn't she? Well, of course she's always bullied Cecily within an inch of her life, and Cecily has let her do it, and this is the result. Frederica simply wouldn't *let* her marry."

"Oh, my dear Theodora," Mrs. Ingram protested, "oughtn't you to have interfered?"

Lady Marlowe shrugged her shoulders.

"If it had been a really good marriage—but one wasn't too keen on it, after all, and as I said to them both, If Cecily is so completely under Frederica's thumb as all that, I really don't think she's fit to marry anybody. She ought to be old enough to know her own mind by this time."

"Do you mean that she just gave it up because Fricky told her to?" Mrs. Ingram asked incredulously.

"Practically. At least I believe there was a tragic scene or two, and the young man was perpetually asking for interviews with me—which I need hardly say he didn't get. Miss Batten saw him, several times—you remember poor old Batten, who's been with us for years and years—and said he was most earnest and melodramatic, and threatened her with Cecily's committing suicide or going off her head. As I said when she told me, he must have a considerably exaggerated idea of his own value!"

Monica moved uneasily.

"Did he—Dr. Corderey—say anything to Frederica?"

"Say anything to Frederica!" echoed Lady Marlowe derisively. "My dear, according to Batten, it was Frederica who did all the saying. She made a fearful scene, and appealed to Cecily in front of him, and told her she'd got to choose between them. Naturally, as Batten said, anyone who knew Cecily would have known perfectly well that she'd never fail Frederica in front of anybody else. It simply isn't in her to do it. She's had this morbid dependence on Fricky all her life and it isn't going to vanish into nothingness at the word of a man she hasn't known more than a few months, as you may

198

suppose. It's been the ruin of Fricky and Cecily," said Lady Marlowe calmly, "that they were never forcibly separated when they were children."

"Then Dr. Corderey was right," Monica said.

Both her seniors stared at her in astonishment.

Then Mrs. Ingram said, "Don't be silly, darling," and Lady Marlowe, raising her eyebrows, asked for another cup of tea.

"Oh, I'm so sorry—do forgive me, Theodora. But really, I've been so absorbed in what you were telling us . . . Well, my dear, what's going to happen now?"

Lady Marlowe emitted her high, unfeeling laugh.

"My dear, all the excitement having died down, and Corderey having been got rid of, the faithful Batten wrote to me —I need not tell you that I'd left the house and gone to stay with the Evelyns, and various other congenial people—and so back I went.

"Cecily was looking like death—but she's always done that at intervals, after all—and Fricky was quite unbearably sulky and injured—God knows why, having got her own way! I simply read them the Riot Act. This, I said, is the last straw. I'm not going to give either of you any more chances. It's no pleasure to me, I said, to be seen about with two young women of nearly six foot high who can't smile, can't talk, can't dance, can't hold themselves properly, and in fact can't do anything at all except make absurd scenes and be intense about one another. It's the thoroughly unnatural, I said, and I'm not in the least surprised that between you, you've managed to put off every man who's ever looked in your direction.

"I'm going to let each of them have an allowance, and they can stay where they are, in the country, with Batten to pick up the pieces when they fight."

Lady Marlowe began to draw on her gloves.

Monica watched her with a kind of dreadful fascination.

Did she know that she was cruel?

"Good-bye, Imogen. Of course, all this is entirely private. I know I can trust you and Monica."

"Of course. We've thought so much about it all."

"Sweet of you, my dear. Well, now you know the whole story. Monica, you must go and stay with them when the weather gets rather nicer, if you wouldn't be too bored. They'd love to have you, I know, and I'm sure you could put a little sense into them if you tried."

She laughed again.

"Really, one's daughters! Not that you're anything but extremely lucky in yours, Imogen—I've a very soft corner for dear little Monica, as you know. I've always said she should have a diamond bracelet as a wedding-present, and so you shall, Monica. Don't leave it too long, my dear."

Lady Marlowe kissed Mrs. Ingram, adjusted her veil in front of the glass, and was seen downstairs to the waiting motor-car by Monica.

When Monica returned to her mother Mrs. Ingram said thoughtfully: "What a cat she is!"

Both of them knew that the reference was to Lady Marlowe's final injunction to Monica, not to leave it too long.

"What utter nonsense, her telling us that it was private about Cecily. As if I didn't know perfectly that Theodora will make a thoroughly good story of it wherever she goes for months to come!"

"I don't see how she can," Monica observed.

"Well, really, I don't know that it isn't the wisest thing she can do. Everyone knows perfectly well how disgusted she is that both the girls have been failures, and so she may just as well make a joke of it. People are anyhow going to say spiteful things, whatever line she takes."

"Yes," said Monica, "I suppose so."

Mrs. Ingram began to replace the cushions on the sofa.

"Ring, darling. This room needs tidying; the newspaper seems to be up here instead of in the library. There's one thing, anyway. Those wretched girls needn't feel that neither of them has ever had a look-in of any kind. Even though it didn't come to anything, Cecily can always tell people that there *has* been a man who definitely did ask her to marry him."

CHAPTER II

ONE DAY Mrs. Ingram unexpectedly said to Monica:
"Is Carol Anderson at all in earnest, darling?"

Monica, startled, did not know how to reply, although she understood perfectly what her mother meant.

"Because if he's not, there's no real use in his continually coming here, and in your going about with him. It may put off other men who might really mean something."

"What other men?" Monica demanded with sudden bitterness. It was Mrs. Ingram's turn to look startled.

"Don't talk like that, darling," she began automatically, and then checked herself as though realizing the futility of her own admonition.

They looked at one another in silence for a moment.

Then Mrs. Ingram turned her eyes away from Monica, and said, in a tone so unwonted that Monica scarcely recognized it as an expression of timidity:

"Naturally I'm only too glad you should have him here. And he's very nice in many ways, though I'm not sure dear father would have thought him good enough for you, quite—I was only just wondering if, perhaps, if he was taking up your time rather unfairly, and not going to be of any real use at the end of it all."

"We're friends, mother. That's all."

"Darling, there's no such thing as friendship between an unmarried man and woman.'"

Monica knew very well that from that Victorian stronghold her mother could never be moved.

She reflected gloomily how true it was that she saw a great deal of Carol, and that it had not led, and probably never would lead, to his asking her to marry him. He was continually inviting her to accompany him to picture-galleries, concerts, plays, and even on expeditions to the country.

He was an agreeable companion, especially when he forgot to try and impress her, and as he became more assured of her liking and sympathy he became more natural with her, and therefore more likeable. Sometimes Monica could succeed in forgetting that she was a woman and Carol a man, and that if she could not make him fall in love with her, it was something between a disgrace and a misfortune.

Nothing could be more evident than that, if he was at all in love with her—which Monica doubted—he did not know it himself, nor ever intend to know it. He was introspective, vain, and imaginative, and not passionate, and his idealization of his affair with Viola Lester appeared to satisfy him emotionally. He still spoke of it, although less frequently, and from time to time worked up a recrudescence of despair, convincing to himself if not to Monica.

It sometimes vaguely crossed her mind that it would be satisfactory to tell Carol the truth about himself, and even to laugh—frankly, and with friendliness—at his childlike self-deceptions, but she was afraid of losing his friendship, and would not risk it. He was her chief outside interest in life, even though she had almost given up hope that he would ever want to marry her.

Monica did not, nowadays, know many unmarried men. She no longer went to dances, and her mother had ceased to entertain.

Mr. Pelham and one or two other middle-aged men still called faithfully upon the widow and her daughter on Sunday afternoons, and once Monica met Claude Ashe, whom she had not seen for years, in the Park.

He talked to her for a little while, looking curiously unaltered, but they had nothing to say to one another, and although she knew that he was not married she felt no wish to meet him again.

It was when she got home, after that encounter, that

Monica deliberately stood and examined her own reflection in the mirror for some time. Something had told her that Claude Ashe, who had once admired her so much, had seen a far greater alteration in her than she had in him.

She sought to discover wherein it lay.

Except that her fresh colour had faded and her hair become a dull, instead of a bright, brown, she could not see any very startling changes in herself. She was thinner, certainly—and the little line between her eyebrows and the faint downward drag at the corners of her mouth had not been there in her early youth.

It wasn't that.

It was something vital, magnetic, that had gone out of her. Something that had attracted men.

Monica caught her breath, and turned away from the mirror.

Day by day, life seemed to her more utterly dreary and devoid of interest. She even thought of trying to find an occupation for herself—visiting a Settlement, or going to help at an East End Club—but she knew that the mere suggestion would distress her mother, who would see in it a public admission of the fact that Monica was a failure.

Vernon Ingram had died in the winter. In the summer following his death, Mrs. Ingram was trying to make up her mind where she and Monica would spend August and September. Various old friends had sent kindly invitations, but Mrs. Ingram could not bear the idea of accepting any of them.

"People mean to be very kind, I know, but there's always something going on in a country house—people coming and going, and young things playing tennis, and perhaps music in the evenings—I couldn't stand it. But you'd better go without me, my darling."

She did not really expect Monica to go without her, as they both knew, and the suggestion was not even seriously discussed between them.

Scotland, where they had always gone before, was declared by Mrs. Ingram to be equally intolerable.

"Everything would remind me so terribly. . . . It would all be just the same, and my life so different, so absolutely changed."

She began to cry.

Evening after evening they went over the same ground. It sometimes seemed to Monica as if her mother did not really want to make up her mind at all. At last she said:

"Why shouldn't we stay in London, and not go away after all?"

"We couldn't stay in London through August, darling. There isn't a soul left. You know that as well as I do. Besides, the servants must have their holidays."

"Shall we try going abroad, somewhere?"

"You and I by ourselves? Darling, you don't understand how difficult it would all be without a man. We've always had dear father to see to everything and take care of us before."

Decision seemed as far off as ever.

Late in July Carol Anderson went to Scotland. He told Monica that he should miss her dreadfully and that they must write very often to one another. He was to be away until September.

"I hope you'll have a good time, Carol, and enjoy yourself," said Monica.

"I don't think I ever enjoy things exactly," said Carol thoughtfully. "To be perfectly honest with you, I never can see that there is anything to enjoy in life."

He gave her his melancholy smile.

"I used not to be like that, of course. I have quite exceptional powers of enjoyment by nature, I believe."

"They'll come back," suggested Monica maliciously.

He shook his head.

"You may be right, my dear, but I don't think so. I'm very peculiar in that way. Other people may change and get over things. I never do."

There seemed no more to be said.

Although Mrs. Ingram had affirmed that Carol Anderson

was of no real use, his departure from London seemed to help her to come to a decision of her own.

She suggested to Monica that it would be nice to take a small house near the New Forest for August and part of September.

Monica agreed, as she would have agreed to any definite plan in her relief at seeing an end to the nightly discussions that never seemed to lead anywhere. She felt grateful to Mr. Pelham who had suggested that plan and had told them of a house that was to let provided the owners—cousins of his own—could find tenants whom they knew, or of whom they knew.

"They would be only too delighted at your taking the little place. It's quite a cottage, most charming, and in the very edge of the Forest. If you don't know that part of the world, Mrs. Ingram, you really ought to go there. But, of course, don't let me persuade you to anything, unless you really feel you'd like it."

Mrs. Ingram did not, like Carol Anderson, protest that she was incapable now of liking anything. She thanked Mr. Pelham, declared definitely that she would write at once to his cousins, and suggested that he should himself come down and spend a few days with them if they did become tenants of the cottage.

Mr. Pelham gravely and gratefully accepted.

Three weeks later, he redeemed his promise.

Monica was a little doubtful as to his entertainment. The cottage was certainly, as he had told them, charming, but life there was very quiet and the chief occupation of the day was to walk in the Forest.

"What on earth shall we do with him if it rains?" she enquired.

"Darling," said her mother impatiently, "it isn't as if he was a very young man. He'll be quite happy with the newspaper indoors, and after dinner we can always play cards, or have a little music. It's delightful to have the use of that good gramophone."

In her gratification at finding a gramophone and a quantity of records, Mrs. Ingram had overcome her inability to listen to music. She said, perhaps truly, that a gramophone was not music.

Her prophecy concerning Mr. Pelham was proved correct.

He was a very easy guest, and in addition the weather was lovely and the Forest more beautiful than Monica could have imagined. It was a beauty that calmed and rested her, even while it made her heart ache in the perpetual loneliness of which she was always conscious, and which the presence of Mr. Pelham at first did little to dispel.

He knew the Forest well, and constituted himself Monica's guide on daily strolls that he invariably referred to as "rambles."

Mrs. Ingram sometimes came with them in the mornings, starting out after eleven and returning very soon after twelve. Lunch was at one, and followed by a dawdling period in the garden or little shady drawing-room, and then Mrs. Ingram went to the room, and Monica and the visitor set out—this time more briskly—sometimes taking with them a picnic tea.

Their conversations were usually impersonal, except when Mr. Pelham embarked on a story—of which he had many—concerning mutual acquaintances. His detailed descriptions and reiterations on these occasions were apt to send Monica into a brown study, from which she roused herself periodically to grasp at the thread of the story, and ejaculate a comment or two.

He never seemed to resent any lack of attention on her part, and gradually Monica perceived that Mr. Pelham was coming to attach a certain sentimental value to their companionship.

She had known him so long, and had thought of him as being so much older than herself, that at first the realization startled her, and she felt disinclined to believe in her own intuitive conviction.

Then her mother suddenly put it into words.

She was alone with Monica in the drawing-room. Through the open French window they could catch a distant glimpse of the top of Mr. Pelham's panama hat showing over the back of a deck-chair, and of the sheets of the morning paper scattered all round him on the lawn. The angle of the deck-chair, no less than the discarded leaves of *The Morning Post*, seemed to indicate that Mr. Pelham was sleeping, after Sunday lunch and a cigarette.

"There's something very simple and nice about him," said Mrs. Ingram abruptly. "After all, it might have been rather awkward, having him here without another man, or anything much to entertain him—but I think he's really quite happy."

"So do I."

"If you come to think of it, he's really one of the oldest friends we've got. At any rate since you grew up."

"I know. I was thinking of that only the other day."

"Were you, darling?" said Mrs. Ingram wistfully.

She looked at her daughter.

"Monica—do you suppose——?"

"No—oh no," said Monica uncertainly. "I'm sure he wouldn't think of anything of that kind. He's not that sort of man, really, is he?"

"It's quite time he settled down."

The phrase, with its implication of a butterfly-like past, was so inappropriate that they both smiled.

"The Marlowes always used to say that he'd been refused by at least six different girls."

"The Marlowes!" ejaculated Mrs. Ingram, with great contempt. "As if the Marlowes knew anything about it! If he'd proposed to one of *them* he wouldn't have been refused, that's very certain."

"I don't think he likes them."

"I've yet to meet the man that does—except, I suppose, Cecily's ridiculous doctor, and she managed to choke *him* off."

"I wish I knew what was happening to poor Cecily."

Mrs. Ingram made no effort to follow Monica's lead, and change the conversation. She remained silent for a few moments and then said:

"After all, he's thoroughly nice and sensible and quite-quite, and father liked him, I remember. You do think him nice, don't you, Monica?"

"Very," said Monica laconically.

She was not in the least preoccupied with any consideration as to whether or not she thought Mr. Pelham nice.

All that she could think of was the exciting, bewildering, fantastic idea that at last, after all these years, she might find herself freed from the stigma of being a woman who had not been sought after by men.

It was incredible.

It was too good to be true.

Monica decided that it was of no use to think about it, and then thought of little else.

She knew that her mother, inwardly, was also profoundly excited.

Mr. Pelham, however, was calm, and gave no sign of any inner perturbation.

On the last evening of his visit it was very hot.

After dinner Mrs. Ingram sat by the open window of the drawing-room, slowly fanning herself. She urged Monica and Mr. Pelham to go out into the garden and seek a breath of air.

"Come too," suggested Monica.

"No, darling, I'd rather sit still. I never knew such heat! I'm sure there's a storm coming."

"I hope not," said Mr. Pelham, "I was going to suggest that we might wander to the edge of the Forest. It would be cool there."

"The dew will be rather heavy, under the trees—but still —only you must take a wrap with you, Monica, my child— one never knows."

"Mother! I *couldn't* catch cold!"

"Girls always say that—but their mothers know better!"

Mrs. Ingram, in an access of archness that caused Monica to flush hotly, looked at Mr. Pelham, as though inviting him to exchange a glance with her over the incredible rashness and ignorance of young girls.

Feeling as though she were being made a fool of, Monica went into the hall and fetched a white serge tennis-coat.

"Allow me," said Mr. Pelham, taking it from her.

Her mother watched them with approving eyes.

"Why not come too?" Mr. Pelham said persuasively.

Instantly Monica felt aggrieved. Did he *want* the company of a third person?

"No, really, thank you. I'm more comfortable resting here."

"We shan't be very long," Monica observed curtly.

She stepped out into the perfect stillness of a summer night.

"*Look* at the stars!"

Mr. Pelham gazed upwards.

" 'Star of the evening, beautiful, beautiful star,' " he said.

They passed down the garden, and outside into the road beyond. Already they were on the edge of the Forest.

The hush was profound.

"Do you think it would be unwise to sit down here for a moment or two? Let me put your coat down for you, to protect your dress."

He carefully laid her coat across a fallen tree-trunk, and Monica sat down upon it. As Mr. Pelham took his place beside her, she was suddenly reminded of the afternoon that she had spent sitting on a fallen tree-trunk with Carol Anderson on a Surrey common.

Monica supposed that she could very easily have fallen in love with Carol. She had been near to it, that day on Hindhead. Afterwards, unacknowledged disappointment had gradually been merged into affection born of understanding, and of his curious dependence on her.

Although the possibility of falling in love with him had been killed, Monica felt that she could have loved Carol warmly and maternally had she become his wife, and that his weakness would neither have angered her nor have roused her contempt. Perhaps, as his sense of security strengthened, he might even have grown away from his childish posturings and pretences. . . .

". . . so that, having made my little confession, I ask you, Monica, most earnestly, if you will become my wife."

Monica was so much startled at the realization that Mr. Pelham was actually proposing to her, and that she had failed to hear anything he had said excepting the last few words, that she nearly fainted.

For an instant, everything swayed round her, and she felt intensely sick.

In a blind, feeble gesture, seeking to steady herself, she put out one hand.

Mr. Pelham gently took it into one of his own, and patted it with the other.

His earnest, prawn-like eyes were fixed upon Monica's face.

"I would do everything I possibly could to try and make you happy. I've thought for some time that we—we should be very well suited to one another, if I may say so. Won't you say Yes, Monica?"

With a flood of incredulous joy and relief, that such a moment should have come to her after all, Monica, in a strangely unsteady voice, answered him.

"Yes."

"You have made me very happy, and done me a great honour," said Mr. Pelham solemnly.

He stood up.

His movements, although lacking in spontaneity, were not uncertain.

After an instant's pause, he bent and kissed Monica's lips once, very deliberately.

The contact neither pleased nor displeased her, although it faintly startled her.

She was thinking of the rapture with which her mother would receive their announcement.

" You have made me very happy," Mr. Pelham repeated. Monica smiled up at him tremulously.

" I'm very happy too," she said simply.

" Shall we stroll a little further? I mustn't let you catch a chill. I shall be taking care of you now, you know."

He helped her up from the log, and then drew her hand through his arm.

"There," said Mr. Pelham, in a tone of satisfaction. "Quite like an old married couple already."

CHAPTER III

Now that she was no longer either unhappy, anxious, or continually conscious of humiliation and failure, Monica was astonished at the rapidity with which she regained a great measure of her lost prettiness.

Life seemed too good to be true.

The days flew by, filled with shopping expeditions, visits to dressmakers, photographers and jewellers, and inspections of possible flats and houses.

Mrs. Ingram was even more radiant than Monica.

She was anxious that the wedding should take place as soon as possible, and a day was fixed, six weeks from the date of Monica's engagement, and announced at the same time.

For a week before the announcement appeared Monica was busy writing to relations, or old friends, who must not be allowed to learn the news first from the columns of *The Morning Post*.

One of the earliest letters that she wrote was to Carol Anderson, in Scotland.

Although she had been faintly in love with him, it was with pure relief that Monica told him of her impending marriage thankfully realizing that she need no longer depend upon the tenuous link that bound them for her sole hope of credit in the eyes of the world.

Carol's answer startled her very much.

He wrote with great brevity, the merest conventional phrase of congratulation, and announced that he should be in London the following week, and must see her immediately.

Could it be possible, she thought, that he was jealous? Monica's newly revived vanity expanded further at the thought, and she allowed her mind to dwell on it for a

moment, wondering what on earth she should do if Carol
came and told her that he loved her, and would not allow
her to marry anybody else.

At once, the question answered itself.

Carol might say, and even believe, that he loved her, but
how far was he to be relied upon?

Herbert Pelham had asked her to marry him. He was in
earnest. He stood for security and, above all, for the removal
of Monica's reproach amongst women.

The years of anxiety and suspense had taught her their
lesson. Not for Carol Anderson, or for anyone or anything
in this world, would Monica relinquish the blessed certainty
of becoming a wife.

She saw Carol alone, in the Eaton Square drawing-room,
about a month before her wedding-day.

She noticed at once that he looked ill, and very unhappy.

"Monica!"

"Carol—I'm so glad to see you."

She hesitated nervously.

"Your letter—didn't seem like you, somehow."

Carol sank into a chair. All his movements, always, were
in keeping with his mood of the moment. His attitude, now,
was plainly intended to denote exhaustion, the lassitude of a
profound discouragement.

He shaded his face with his hand, and said nothing.

"Were you surprised at my news?" Monica enquired,
anxious to come quickly to the issue.

"Naturally. You'd said nothing about it, had you?"

"Carol! How could I? There was no question—I didn't
really know anything about it myself, till it happened."

Carol took down his hand and looked at Monica with a
look that she could not help thinking he himself felt to be a
peculiarly piercing one.

"Is that the *truth*?"

"Of course it is."

He threw himself back again in his arm-chair and said
abruptly:

213

"I believe you. I didn't know before—but I do believe you now."

"I should hope you do. Will you tell me what's the matter, please?"

Monica's new-born self-assurance had unconsciously communicated itself to her voice and manner. For the first time she was speaking to Carol without regard for his susceptibilities, or his supposed reaction to her words.

"What do you imagine is the matter?" Carol enquired bitterly. "You've let me down utterly, Monica—you've failed me—and I trusted you."

She felt dizzy with surprise and perplexity.

"How? How have I failed you?"

"Monica! Don't pretend. How can we go on being friends, as we have been, once you're married? You know perfectly well it will be out of the question. It wouldn't be fair on Pelham to begin with, and I don't suppose he'd even allow it. Naturally."

"But, Carol—of course we can still be friends. I don't see why it need make any difference."

Monica spoke without conviction, partly because she did not really believe what she was saying, and partly because she was still utterly undecided as to whether Carol did, or did not, mean that he had wanted to marry her himself.

Carol was very quick to see, and take, the advantage that her uncertainty gave him.

"You're not being honest with me. You know perfectly well that on the day you promised to marry another man you were virtually giving me up."

"But I——" Monica hesitated, helpless.

"You can't possibly deny it," Carol asserted. "And I think that you do, at least, owe me absolute sincerity, Monica. That's why your letter hurt me so frightfully. You wrote, didn't you, pretending to think that I shouldn't mind, that I could let you go quite easily and happily. Yet you must have known that it wasn't so."

"Honestly, Carol, I——"

"My dear, I know exactly what you're going to say. I know just how you've reasoned it out, in your own thoughts, persuading yourself that it would be all right, and that we could go on as before. You may be able to deceive yourself, Monica, but it's impossible for you to deceive me. That's a thing that nobody has ever succeeded in doing."

Monica stared at him, utterly impotent in the face of his astonishing belief in himself and his own words.

"I'm pretty certain," Carol went on, "that I understand you a great deal better than you understand yourself. I can see, for instance, how this has happened. We hadn't seen each other for some weeks, and you're the sort of person—and I'm not saying this at all unkindly—with whom it's rather, Out of sight out of mind. Your friendship for me probably weakened, simply because I wasn't there, beside you."

"You've no right to——"

"Yes, I have. I've every right. We've been friends all this time, I've given you more of my confidence than I ever have to any other woman, and I've helped you to the very best of my ability. I'm not going to pretend to you that I don't know I've done something for you, in the past two years. I've given you the very best I had to give, Monica, and you're flinging it all back in my face."

His voice broke.

"But Carol," said Monica desperately, "you don't mean that—you weren't ever—you wouldn't ever have fallen in love with me yourself, would you?"

She felt that she was expressing herself crudely, and even grossly, and gave the words a downward inflection that made them sound like an assertion, rather than a question.

He turned and looked at her quickly, and Monica realized that for a moment she had disconcerted him. He had not yet acquired an attitude of mind with which to meet her suggestion.

He spoke only after an uncomfortable moment's pause.

"It's perfectly impossible, my dear, to say what might or

might not have happened. You must know that, as well as I do. There's only one woman in the world that I love, or ever shall love. I've always told you so. Other people may change; I never shall. I'm like that. But what you're doing is hurting me abominably. You're not only taking yourself away from me, you're taking away my faith in women. Monica, ask yourself honestly if you think you have any right to do that."

Monica understood that Carol was willing to relinquish neither his original claim to a *grande passion* for Viola Lester, nor his newly evolved grievance against herself. With an ingenuity that only a flawless degree of self-deception could have achieved, he had contrived to reconcile two aspects of himself that must, under less skilful handling, have appeared as mutually destructive one of the other.

It would be not only useless, but also very nearly impossible, to try and make him face reality.

Monica stood up.

"I'm very, very sorry," she said, with finality.

Carol stood up too, and he had, under the stress of his self-induced emotion, turned white.

"You understand that it's good-bye, Monica?"

"If you feel that it must be. I don't. And perhaps some day——"

"If I go now, you won't see me again."

Monica hesitated for a moment, and then held out her hand to him.

"Very well," said Carol hoarsely.

With knit brows and compressed lips he gazed at her, and then, unexpectedly, kissed her forehead, with a long, solemn kiss.

"Good-bye, Monica. God bless you."

She made no answer, and, with squared shoulders, Carol Anderson marched out of the room, without looking back. Monica felt sure that he was making exactly the exit that he visualized himself as making.

She did not feel convinced that his farewell was destined to be a final one, and in effect she received three letters from him, in quick succession, within the week. All were long, involved, reproachful, and conceived in a spirit of ardent self-pity.

In the midst of her new preoccupations and interests there was but little time to write replies. Monica sent one answer, that she herself felt to be a cursory and uninspired production, and then wrote no more. She forgot Carol so readily and so completely, that it did not even occur to her as strange that she should have done so.

Nothing, now, was of the least importance excepting her wedding preparations, and the long-desired and despaired-of honour that was now hers.

Her mother's happiness was almost as great as Monica's, and far more freely expressed.

"It's everything that I could have wished," she declared to all her oldest friends and numerous relations. "We've known Herbert for years, and dear Vernon used to like him, and say how sound he was in all his views. I've no doubts whatever about his making Monica happy, and of course it's too delightful that she'll be living in London, so that I shan't feel I've lost her in the least."

"Very unselfish of you, Imogen," observed old cousin Blanche. "I'm afraid you'll be lonely, all the same, when she's gone, even if it's only into the next street."

"Never mind," said Mrs. Ingram radiantly. "It's the fate of a mother, isn't it? I always knew I couldn't hope to keep Monica always with me, though she's been a very devoted, unselfish child. I daresay you've guessed that there have been one or two little episodes, before this happened—but she wouldn't hear of leaving me. And, of course, one felt that none of them were quite the real thing, so far as she herself was concerned. *This*, I'm thankful to say, is very different."

The days rushed by, filled with appointments, letters, presents, preparations.

"I hope you're not wearing yourself out," said Mr. Pelham solicitously, two days, before the wedding.

Monica laughed and shook her head.

217

"You certainly look remarkably well."

A faint expression of admiration was visible in his bulging, prawn-eyes, and Monica felt a rush of gratitude, and of trembling pride at having inspired it.

A house had been found in Beaufort Gardens, and was to be painted and decorated whilst the bridal couple were spending their honeymoon in Italy. Monica and Mr. Pelham, tacitly and without discussion, had agreed that Beaufort Gardens was quite near enough to Eaton Square.

They looked forward to furnishing their house and installing themselves in it on their return.

"Why, we shall be quite an old married couple by that time," Mr. Pelham playfully observed.

Monica found it difficult to believe.

One night she dreamed that it had all been a mistake about her marriage, and that she was not engaged at all. She woke, sweating and sobbing, to an intense wave of relief as her fingers sought and found the big half-hoop of diamonds on her left hand.

It was on the following night, the one before her wedding-day, that her mother came softly into her room, after Monica had already been in bed for nearly an hour.

Monica, who had not been to sleep, sat up.

"Lie down again, darling. I didn't want to disturb you— we want you to look your best to-morrow, and you must get plenty of sleep to-night."

As she spoke, Mrs. Ingram took her accustomed seat on the side of the bed.

"My pet, I can scarcely believe it's your wedding-day to-morrow. It seems only the other day that you were a little thing in the nursery, peeping at me through the bars of your cot when I came upstairs to see you before going out to a dinner-party."

"I can remember a lovely pink evening dress you used to wear, with puffed sleeves," said Monica smiling.

She found it easier to speak of her baby days to her mother than of the later years.

218

"If only *dear* father could have known about this—it would have made him so happy!" mourned Mrs. Ingram.

"I wish he had," said Monica, with the pang that would always come at the recollection of her father's unspoken disappointment and mortification that his daughter had not been sought in marriage.

"But after all, he did know Herbert, and liked him very much."

"Yes," said Mrs. Ingram quickly. "I always think it's such a good sign when a man is popular with other men. You see, they can judge of one another so much better than we can."

"I suppose they can."

"I feel that Herbert is so absolutely reliable."

"Yes," Monica agreed, "that's one of the things one likes so much about him."

"You needn't be nervous, with a man of his kind—and one whom you've known so long. Though I must say, I rather like a bride to look nervous. Your dress is *perfect*, Monica."

"I can't believe," said Monica, "that it's really there, hanging up in the wardrobe—my wedding-dress."

Her mother pressed her hand.

"I hope the little bridesmaids will behave nicely, and manage your train properly."

Monica had decided to have child-attendants. Almost all her contemporaries were married, and she did not want grown-up bridesmaids who would yet be several years younger than she was herself. It had all been understood between herself and her mother without any need for words. Two little Ingram cousins had been invited to officiate, and their father was to give Monica away.

Mrs. Ingram began to enumerate various small aspects of the great event—Monica's new jewel-case, that had been promised from the shop for that afternoon and hadn't yet arrived—the bunches of roses for the bridesmaids—her own *toilette* of silver-grey and lavender—and the arrangements made for the breakfast after the ceremony.

Although she had been living in the atmosphere of exactly such preparations for days past, Monica listened with a sense of incredulous astonishment that they should concern herself. It still seemed absolutely impossible that the miracle should have happened.

"I'm glad poor Fricky and Cecily are coming down for your wedding," pursued Mrs. Ingram, in a tone of indulgent superiority.

"I hope it won't upset Cecily."

"Well, darling, she had her chance, and didn't know how to make the most of it. I'm sorry for poor Theodora, I must say. Neither of them will ever marry now, of course."

"I wish they could. I'd like them to be happy." Monica, now, could afford to be generous.

"In a country where there aren't enough men to go round girls have got to take trouble if they want lives of their own," observed Mrs. Ingram simply. "Frederica and Cecily never took the least trouble to attract men, even when they were quite young—and look at the result! I'm sorry for their poor mother."

"She hasn't really been very nice to them, ever."

Since her engagement, Monica had found herself licensed to criticize her seniors in a hitherto unprecedented manner.

"No, I don't think she has," Mrs. Ingram admitted. "But after all, one must remember that it's a bitter disappointment for a woman to have two daughters, and no son at all."

There was a silence. Monica wondered whether her mother's thoughts had taken the same direction as had her own.

Mrs. Ingram stooped and kissed her.

"Good-night, my darling. God bless you. I mustn't keep you awake any longer."

Monica was touched at her mother's self-restraint in not having said a word about her own loneliness when her daughter should be gone.

She put her arms round her neck, as she had not done since childhood.

"You won't miss me too much, will you? I shall be quite

close by, you know, and it'll be such fun showing you the house and everything. You won't feel too lonely?"

"No, no. I shall be all right. Nothing in the world could make me happier than to see you safely married to a good man—and a gentleman—someone we've known almost all our lives, like Herbert."

They kissed, stirred by unusual emotions.

Suddenly Monica felt her mother's hot tears on her face.

"Darling," whispered Mrs. Ingram brokenly, "it isn't what we once dreamed of for you—it isn't as if—— But oh, Monica, say you'll be happy. I couldn't, couldn't have borne to see you an old maid."

Monica could not answer.

She pressed her mother more closely in her arms.

At last she said, in a stifled murmur:

"It's all right, mother—really. I'm very happy."

It was true.

Monica was happier than she had ever thought to be, since the far-off days of her unshattered, youthful confidence.

For the first time since her foolish love-affair with Christopher Lane, Monica had regained her self-respect.

It was Monica's wedding-day.

She was moving slowly up the aisle, veiled and robed in white, to the pealing of the organ, just as she had so often, waking and sleeping, dreamed of doing.

The tightly-frock-coated form of her bridegroom stood at the chancel rails, a white flower correctly decorating his button-hole, his hand nervously smoothing the thin, dark strands that lay sparsely across the crown of his head.

Monica did not really see him.

She did not see her mother in the front bench, already sobbing in a quiet ecstasy, nor cousin Blanche craning anxiously forward under her huge flowered hat.

She did not see Frederica and Cecily Marlowe, the resemblance between them now strangely accentuated until each looked merely the pale shadow of a pale shadow.

She did not see Carol Anderson, who stood with folded arms and compressed lips, gazing at her with a fixed look of mingled reproach and fortitude.

Monica saw nothing. She was conscious of nothing, save that the moment towards which the whole of life had been tending had come at last.

As she knelt at the chancel steps, her heart was filled with a prayer of ardent and humble thanksgiving.

She was to have a life of her own, after all.

A home, a husband, a recognized position as a married woman—an occupation. At last, she would have justified her existence.

Up to the very last moment she had been afraid, and had known that her mother was afraid, lest something should happen to prevent her marriage.

Nothing had happened: she was safe for ever.

There was no further need to be afraid, or ashamed, or anxious, any more.

She prayed that she might be a good wife to Herbert, and that if ever they had a child it might be a son.

AFTERWORD

"Thank Heaven, fasting, for a good man's love" is Rosalind's sharp rejoinder, in *As You Like It*, to the proud shepherdess. As advice it is ambiguous, because Rosalind can only give it while she is passing herself off as a man. And E.M. Delafield's book, delightful (like everything she wrote) to read, is not as straightforward as it looks at first.

Most recollections of E.M. Delafield are of the handsome countrywoman and J.P., organizing and well organized, the competent mother, the successful public speaker, a director of *Time and Tide*. "A witty, extremely *soignée* person" an American interviewer found her in 1942. One might not have guessed that her sympathies were with the Labour Party, and there are other unexpected glimpses of her, for example on her visits to Russia where she had arranged to meet the young journalist Peter Stucley. "With a hat" he wrote, "from Marshall & Snelgrove on her head, and in her hand a bag which always contained, at moments of exhaustion, a supply of ginger biscuits" they toured Moscow together, although their last outing, to a reformatory for prostitutes, was cancelled. In her own account she describes how she washed his handkerchiefs and saw him off "in deepest dejection", feeling like *l'orpheline de Moscou*. The total impression— and this, I believe, accounts for the comic and pathetic tension of her books—is of a woman who would like to free herself and understands how it is to be done but can never quite bring herself to the point of doing it. "Realize, not for the first time," writes the Provincial Lady,* "that intelligent women can perhaps best

*E.M. Delafield, *The Diary of a Provincial Lady*, Virago Modern Classics, 1984.

perform their duty towards their own sex by devastating process of telling them the truth about themselves. At the same time, cannot feel that I shall really enjoy hearing it." What held her back—and she knew this, of course, better than anyone—was partly inborn, partly imposed. At convent school, she said, she had been taught for life that "a good reason for doing something was that I knew I should hate it". An even stronger influence was her mother.

This mother was also a novelist. Mrs Henry de la Pasture had a great popular following, and when Elizabeth began to publish she called herself Delafield (a translation of sorts), apparently to keep clear of her mother's success. Why not, however, a different name altogether? Mrs de la Pasture's books went into many editions, including Newnes' Sixpenny Novels and Hodder and Stoughton's Sevenpenny Library. Among her titles are *The Grey Knight: An Autumn Love Story* (1908) and *The Lonely Lady of Grosvenor Square* (1907). Her advice to her daughter was to write about something of which she had personal experience, but in her own novels this experience is certainly heightened. You get dash and spirit from Mrs de la Pasture, and generous wish-fulfilment. Her heroines are the middle-aged enchantresses dear to middle-aged women authors. Take Lady Mary in *Peter's Mother* (1905). She is a widow, pale, sad, but still beautiful, and free at last to marry her first love. But her son comes back wounded from the Boer War and expects her to make a home for him. When she asks, in a sudden outburst, whether she doesn't deserve a life of her own, she meets total incomprehension. What is disconcerting is to find that in E.M. Delafield's last novel, *Late and Soon* (1943) the same situation appears, though in more painful terms. The Provincial Lady notes "*Mem*: a mother's influence, if any, almost always entirely disastrous." The struggle to escape from it, however, greatly strengthens the critical faculty.

Thank Heaven Fasting was published in 1932, when E.M. Delafield had been writing for twelve years. The period of the story is not precisely given (the First World War is never mentioned), but in Eaton Square the power of money, parental authority and social status is still absolute. Power needs force to support it, and it

224

is the overwhelming force of received opinion which divides the All Right from the Not Quite and makes the unmarried woman something worse than odd—a failure, a disgrace to herself and to what in racing would be called her "connections". The term is the right one, because the young women are bred and trained entirely with the object of getting them successfully married within three years, after which they are regarded, and regard themselves, as leftovers. Grotesquely artificial as the system is, it is biologically predictable. The All Right—even if some of them are Only Just— must reproduce themselves with the All Right to maintain the species. In itself this is a bizarre spectacle, one of nature's processes gone hopelessly astray, which must lead eventually to extinction.

The story opens on a note of keen irony. "Much was said in the days of Monica's early youth about being good." (Monica was one of E.M. Delafield's own names and one may guess that she would rather not have been given it.) Goodness, in this context, means what is convenient to those in authority. Certainly, it has nothing to do with truth. Monica has been carefully trained to behave to men—beginning with her own father—exactly as they expect, and to say to them only what they want to hear.

"Have you been to play whist at the Club, father?"
The question dated from Monica's nursery days. She asked it several times weekly, and never realized that it was a matter of complete indifference to her.

At her first dance she catches sight of herself in one of the great ballroom mirrors and "saw that she was wearing too serious an expression. Both her mother and the dancing-mistress had warned her about this, and she immediately assumed an air of fresh, sparkling enjoyment." At home, after dinner, she sometimes plays the piano

"That will do now, darling," said Mrs Ingram. "I can hear father coming, and he may want to talk. Ring for coffee."
Monica obeyed.
She was not really particularly interested in either the *Adieux* or *Sobre les Olas*, although she vaguely liked the idea of herself, in a simple white frock,

dreamily playing under the lamplight and it always rather annoyed her that her conception of her own appearance had to be spoilt by the fact that, having no faculty for playing by ear, she was obliged always to keep her eyes fixed upon her music.

Monica, then, is not a protester. She is conscious of the duties of her station as a young girl and accepts them without question. All time is wasted—so too is all friendship and all music—unless it can be shown to "lead to something", that is, a proposal of marriage, although it is assumed that the man is likely to try and get out of it if he can. If the offer is not made within the first three seasons, the daughter will have to share with her mother the cruel burden of guilt. Fathers can distance themselves; mothers, if they have failed, must live with failure.

A possible exception to this rule is the handsome, formidable Lady Marlowe (her first husband had been a German Jew, but her second had been English, "so that was all right"). If her two daughters, Frederica and Cicely, prove unattractive to men, Lady Marlowe intends, so she frankly says, to banish them to a separate house and disown them. But such strength, and indeed such cruelty, can hardly be expected of all mothers, nor is it surprising that Frederica and Cicely droop, with dark shadows under their eyes and "pale, inefficient hands".

Monica does not have to suffer from this kind of brutal contempt. The novel would be very much weakened if she did, since another irony of the opening chapters is that her prospects seem so hopeful. She starts out with the goodwill of the entire household, although she knows very little about some of them— "she had a dim idea that the kitchenmaid did actually sleep in the boxroom". She is crimped and squeezed into the desirable shape and launched into the drawing-room world. Once there, her first conversation on her own is a success. She has been able, for several minutes, to think of something to say to a man. It looks, then, as if she will be able to justify her existence and the fact that she was not born a boy. Her parents, who remind her so frequently of all they are doing for her, will not have to be disappointed.

Every now and then E.M. Delafield indicates briefly (she is a very economical writer) how much human material is being wasted or suppressed. Left to herself, Monica has a good heart and a healthy capacity for normal happiness. She loves dancing for its own sake, and, disastrously, she loves Captain Christopher Lane. At his appearance on the scene her eighteen years of training, social, emotional and religious, collapse at a touch. "God must understand her, and must not allow her mother to guess anything at all." Captain Lane, to be sure, is not altogether real to her—"he was masterful, exactly like people in books"—but he is also a powerful physical presence which has nothing to do with books. At the funfair—a strong metaphor for sexual excitement—she finds that she has forgotten her mother and her friends and, as the evening goes on, even time itself. She will never be allowed the chance to do such a thing again. Almost at once time reasserts its power, and becomes a threat. Although the flashy Captain only finds the opportunity for a few kisses before he is posted back to India, Monica's reputation for niceness has gone. She has lost her marketable freshness. She and her mother will be left to count the anxious years as they pass. They are not quite hopeless, but their hopes will be pitched sadly lower and lower.

"The Anxious Years" is the title of the second, and by far the longest part of the novel. Monica, Mrs Ingram and Parsons, the faithful lady's maid, are left in a kind of unholy alliance to keep up appearances in Eaton Square. Monica, once a devourer of fiction, now creates it, inventing, with her mother, new variations of the true story. "They displayed for one another's benefit a detached brightness that ignored everything below the surface," conscious, day in, day out, of "an undercurrent of sick envy and mortification". E.M. Delafield calls their pretence "gallant" as they go through the daily formalities of dressing, shopping, driving out and back home again, which are all they know and which it would never occur to them to give up. Without these things their life would not be endurable.

The men who are supposed to give meaning to their lives are a poor lot, almost all of them self-satisfied and self-deceiving. But the thin characterization of the men, in this particular novel, works

227

very well. They are to be seen as a necessary condition of life rather than as human beings. Poor Monica is patronized by her father, sexually awakened and then ditched by the Captain, disillusioned by Carol Anderson, without understanding any of them. It could be said, indeed, that the true marriage, as the story works itself out, is between Monica and her mother. They have "the intuition peculiar to those who live together". From Monica's first childish dependence she grows into the desperate conspiracy of the middle chapters, until almost imperceptibly she becomes the stronger of the two. "Darling, there's no such thing as friendship between a man and a woman," is Mrs Ingram's comment when Carol Anderson appears, but for the first time her voice is timid. Her last resort is the pretence that she can't bring herself to let her daughter marry and leave her by herself. "Not that I'd ever grudge you your happiness, my precious one, but just for a few years more—I don't suppose it'll be for very long." And Monica, listening, feels "sick with pity".

Earlier in the book she has been jealous of the affection between her parents, and when Vernon Ingram is killed in an accident she envies her mother's hysteria, her right, so to speak, to violent grief. Jealousy, in the peculiarly English form of accepted defeat (everyone else is more fortunate and more worthy of being fortunate) was of particular interest to E.M. Delafield. Unlike lechery and greed, it can never provide satisfaction in itself, only in the thought of someone else's failure. In creating character, she held that

to show one side only is to falsify it, and therefore deprive it of all value . . . there are no wholly "nice" people, or wholly "nasty" people in real life, and they therefore have no place in the particular form of *roman psychologique* in which I happen to be interested.

The jealousy which bedevils the gentle and pliant Monica is a product of "the whole tradition of her world, daily and hourly soaking into her very being, so that it became an ineradicable part of herself". There is, for example, the beginning of a real friendship between Monica and Cicely Marlowe. But the news of Cicely's

228

engagement (even though the man is not All Right) while Monica herself is still doggedly waiting and hoping, is almost too painful to be born. "It added to her misery that she was ashamed of it, and despised and reproached herself for her unworthy jealousy." Still more disgraceful is her relief when the whole thing, after all, comes to nothing.

Thank Heaven Fasting would be a sombre book if it was less witty, and less deceptively mild. Proceeding, as it does, in the kind of short paragraphs which were then thought suitable for the Woman's Page, it concentrates from beginning to end, and with admirable clearness, on the main story. In this sense, it must be counted a classic. Characters and places are carefully limited. The tone is detached, or seems so. E.M. Delafield had, she said, "consciously striven, throughout the whole of my writing life, for ability to observe impartially, unbiassed either by sentiment or by cynicism, and courage to record faithfully and without dramatic emphasis". She isn't impartial, of course. What is the use of an impartial novelist? But she is accurate, calm and lucid. She possessed what she called a phonographic memory, and could repeat, word for word, conversations which she had heard or overheard many years earlier. Dialogue, even in short snatches, is one of her great strengths as a writer. In *Thank Heaven Fasting* the conversations are often—as they are in real life—duels, open or disguised. Mrs Ingram has an easy victory over Monica.

"Sit down, my pet."
"I'd rather stand."
"Mother said, Sit down, Monica."
Monica sat.

The neurotic Frederica also challenges her mother, together with the whole system to which she has been condemned.

"I don't want to get married. I hate men. I wouldn't marry anyone— whoever it was."
Lady Marlowe gazed at her in astonishment for a moment, and then laughed again.
"So you've got to that stage, have you?" was all she said.

And Frederica, left alone, sinks her teeth into the flesh of her thin wrist to control herself. At the other end of the scale is Mr Pelham, amiably chatting on one of his punctual calls.

"The other day" remarked Mr Pelham, "I heard of a fellow who was sitting out a dance with a girl. They'd talked about all the usual things and didn't seem to have anything more to say, and whatever he asked her she only seemed to answer Yes or No—so what do you think he suddenly did?"

"What?"

"He suddenly asked her: 'Do you like string?' Without any preliminary, you know."

Monica smiles, though only because she sees that she is expected to. But she understands as well as he does that between people who are obliged to talk, but have nothing to say, anecdotes, even about string, are precious currency. There is something touching, however, about Mr Pelham's admiration of the resourceful fellow, whom he doesn't even know, but has "heard of". Mr Pelham is tedious—he is the sort of man who always calls a walk "a ramble"—but in his voice one can distinguish human kindness.

If E.M. Delafield had a good ear, she also had an exceptionally sharp eye for—(to quote one of her own titles)—The Way Things Are. The house in Eaton Square dominates *Thank Heaven Fasting*. In Monica's bedroom

The furniture itself was all painted white, so was the narrow little mantelpiece on which stood the collection of china animals dating from nursery days. The pictures were framed in gilt—mostly "copies from the flat" of Swiss scenery, and Italian peasantry, but there were also reproductions of one or two "really *good*" pictures. These had been given to Monica from time to time, usually on birthdays, and she always felt that she ought to have liked them much better than she really did.

In a rebellious moment she had wanted to take down the Sistine Madonna, but had not been able to summon the courage. Her upbringing has taught her that nothing must be taken more seriously than appearances. When she goes to her mother's room after a party "to tell her all about it", she sees the night-time Mrs

230

Ingram, with whom she is quite familiar—her hair in a double row of steel wavers, her face glistening with cold cream, recruiting her forces for the next day's grand pretence. Heavy meals come up from the basement kitchen, clothes are worn which can't be taken off without the help of a servant, fires blaze, bells are rung, hairdressers arrive by appointment—every morning and evening bring the spoils of a comfortable unearned income. It is the only home Monica has ever known, and we have to see it turn first into a refuge for the unwanted, and then into a prison.

In *Thank Heaven Fasting* E.M. Delafield returned to a theme she had treated much earlier, in *Consequences* (1919). In this novel, which was one of her own favourites, the heroine, Alex, is as naive as Monica, but much less able to do what is expected of her. She has suffered—unlike Monica, but like E.M. Delafield herself—from years of spiritual regimentation in a strict Belgian convent. Emerging, bewildered, at the age of eighteen she finds that her parents expect her?—what else has she been growing up for?—to get married. She accepts a proposal from a man she doesn't love, and who removes his pince-nez, with deliberation, before he kisses her. (This is also true of Mr Pelham and of Cecil Vyse in *A Room with a View*; it seems to be an Edwardian novelist's warning signal.) With very real courage, Alex breaks off the engagement. In consequence, her mother's world rejects her. She is undirected, untrained, thought to be odd and difficult. Her brother and sister do not want her, and as a last solution she drowns herself. Monica's story, then, could be seen as a revised version of Alex's; we must accept that comedy is crueller than tragedy. It is interesting to see how E.M. Delafield has quietly removed what might be called the extenuating circumstances. Alex dies because her sincerity is unforgiveable. Monica retreats to the pretences of Eaton Square. Nanda, in Henry James' *The Awkward Age* (who becomes unmarriageable because she is thought to have read a daring book), is shown as finer than all the men and women around her. Monica is not. Gissing's Odd Women lose their means of support. Monica remains comfortably off. In a conforming society, she is a conformist. Her claim to sympathy is only that.

And the reader does sympathize with Monica, all the more because she is unheroic, and finds it almost unbearable when, at the very end of the book, she wakes sweating and sobbing, afraid that after all there may be some hitch to prevent her marriage. One feels almost ashamed to be seeing her desperation at such close range. Was she capable of acting otherwise than as she did? So tightly does her world close around her that it seems, at first, that there are no choices open to her. She has heard faintly of alternatives—the New Woman, the suffrage movement—but she has been taught to regard them with horror, and is duly horrified. Lady Marlowe considers that women who demand votes are simply hysterical old maids, or wives who can't get on with their husbands (she herself has worn out two). No New Women make an appearance (there is a hint of one in Mary Collier, who wears her hair straight and her clothes plain, but it is not developed) and there are no female salary earners—not even writers—among Monica's acquaintance. At one point in the novel, however, when Cicely falls ill, the Marlowes call in young Dr Corderey (clever, but not All Right). Corderey has studied the unhappiness of idle women, and considers it an illness. They need treatment, he thinks, as much as any other patients. To Monica he says

"I suppose you were never sent to school either, and you live at home, and have nothing to do ... and if you were forced to earn your living to-morrow, you'd have to starve."
Monica, for an instant, felt offended, because she knew that her mother would think she ought to be offended. But he had spoken with so much sincerity that she could not pretend to disagree.
"It's quite true."

Monica is listening here to the voice of truth. She has heard it before, more than once. She heard it when she wanted to take down the print of the Sistine Madonna. She expresses it, if only for a moment, when she cries out "Why can't one have a career, or even work, like a man?" She knows that her mother's grief has turned into self-indulgence. She has the capacity even to know herself, but what she sees dismays her. Better to look away. Here

232

E.M. Delafield is relentless. We are not allowed to question the happiness of the happy ending. Quite against the tradition of comedy, the older generation has been proved, apparently, right. And all Monica has to wish for is that if ever she has a child, it will be a boy.

Penelope Fitzgerald, London, 1987

VIRAGO MODERN CLASSICS

The first Virago Modern Classic, *Frost in May* by Antonia White, was published in 1978. It launched a list dedicated to the celebration of women writers and to the rediscovery and reprinting of their works. Its aim was, and is, to demonstrate the existence of a female tradition in fiction which is both enriching and enjoyable. The Leavisite notion of the 'Great Tradition', and the narrow, academic definition of a 'classic', has meant the neglect of a large number of interesting secondary works of fiction. In calling the series 'Modern Classics' we do not necessarily mean 'great'— although this is often the case. Published with new critical and biographical introductions, books are chosen for many reasons: sometimes for their importance in literary history; sometimes because they illuminate particular aspects of womens' lives, both personal and public. They may be classics of comedy or storytelling; their interest can be historical, feminist, political or literary.

Initially the Virago Modern Classics concentrated on English novels and short stories published in the early decades of this century. As the series has grown it has broadened to include works of fiction from different centuries, different countries, cultures and literary traditions. In 1984 the Victorian Classics were launched; there are separate lists of Irish, Scottish, European, American, Australian and other English-speaking countries; there are books written by Black women, by Catholic and Jewish women, and a few relevant novels by men. There is, too, a companion series of Non-Fiction Classics constituting biography, autobiography, travel, journalism, essays, poetry, letters and diaries.

By the end of 1988 over 300 titles will have been published in these two series, many of which have been suggested by our readers.

Also by E. M. Delafield

DIARY OF A PROVINCIAL LADY

"*November 7th* – Plant the indoor bulbs. Just as I am in the middle of them, Lady Boxe calls. I say, untruthfully, how nice to see her. . ."

Thus begins this delightful, witty record of daily life in a Devonshire village between the wars. Through the eyes of the Provincial lady – one of the most enchanting heroines in mid-twentieth century literature – we meet her husband Robert (usually asleep behind *The Times*); her children Robin and Vicky and their very Gallic "Mademoiselle". We meet, too, Lady Boxe (who always calls at the Wrong Moment); Our Vicar and Our Vicar's Wife; and all their friends and neighbours.

Published here are *Diary of a Provincial Lady* (1930) and its three wonderful sequels: *The Provincial Lady Goes Further* (1932), *The Provincial Lady in America* (1934) and *The Provincial Lady in Wartime* (1940). For the life of our heroine does not stop at hearth and home as, a minor literary celebrity, she struggles hilariously for a life of her own in a London flat; goes on a lecture tour of America; and, donning trousers, prepares to "Stand By" and "Do Her Bit" in Hitler's War.

Also by E. M. Delafield

THE WAY THINGS ARE

" 'You've never told me about your marriage,
Laura?' said Duke Ayland.
. . . 'Yes. It's only – I'm very fond of Alfred,' said
Laura, taking the plunge and temporarily unaware
that almost all wives begin conversations about
almost all husbands in precisely the same way' "

Laura has been married for seven years. On those
occasions when an after-dinner snooze behind *The
Times* seems preferable to her riveting conversation
about their two small sons, Laura dismisses the
notion that Alfred does not understand her,
reflecting instead that they are what is called happily
married. At thirty-four, Laura wonders if she's ever
been in love – a ridiculous thing to ask oneself. Then
Duke Ayland enters her life and that vexing question
refuses to remain unanswered . . . With Laura, beset
by perplexing decisions about the supper menu, the
difficulties of appeasing Nurse, and the necessity
of maintaining face within the small village of
Quinnerton, E. M. Delafield created her first
"Provincial Lady". And in the poignancy of Laura's
doubts about her marriage, she presents a dilemma
which many women will recognise.

Also of interest

Pamela Frankau

THE WILLOW CABIN

"He came over to her chair, pulled her out of it and stood holding her hands.

'If I were really grown-up now, I should say good-bye to you and walk out of your life. And yet I cannot bear to go'"

Caroline is twenty-two, gamine and vociferous, neither daunted nor impressed by the prospect of a promising stage career. Then she meets Michael Knowles, a successful middle-aged surgeon, and her career slips into second place beside brief meetings, midnight trysts and the welcome anonymity of foreign cities, as they seek to evade the shadow of Mercedes, Michael's estranged wife. London of the 1930s gives way to the Blitz and the pain of separation and the intensity of wartime does nothing to deflect Caroline's obsession with the three-cornered relationship. In America, some years later, she meets Mercedes for the first time. Discovering an unexpected bond with her, Caroline begins to comprehend her own misinterpretation of the past . . .

Pamela Frankau

A WREATH FOR THE ENEMY

"'In my youth . . . I had an overwhelming passion to be like other people. Other People were a whole romantic race, miles beyond my reach. Not now. I don't really think that they exist, except in the eye of the beholder'"

When Penelope Wells, precocious daughter of a poet, meets the well-behaved middle-class Bradley children, it is love at first sight. But their parents are horrified by the Wells' establishment — a distinctly bohemian hotel on the French Riviera — and the friendship ends in tears. Out of these childhood betrayals grow Penelope, in love with an elusive ideal of order and calm, and Don Bradley, in rebellion against the philistine values of his parents. Compellingly told in a series of first-person narratives, their stories involve them with the Duchess, painted and *outré*; the crippled genius Crusoe; Crusoe's brother Livesey, and the eccentric Cara, whose brittle and chaotic life collides explosively with Penelope's.

"Pamela Frankau uses a large canvas with great deftness, and her dialogue is a joy" — *Sunday Times*